North Carolina Curiosities

North Carolina Curiosities

*Jerry Bledsoe's
Outlandish Guide to
the Dadblamedest Things
to See and Do
in North Carolina*

Second Edition

A Voyager Book

The Globe Pequot Press

Chester, Connecticut

Library of Congress Cataloging-in-Publication Data

Bledsoe, Jerry.
North Carolina curiosities : Jerry Bledsoe's outlandish guide to the dadblamedest things to see and do. – 2nd ed.
    p.   cm.
  "A Voyager book."
  Includes index.
  ISBN 0-87106-528-2
  1. North Carolina – Description and travel – 1981– Guide-books.
2. Curiosities and wonders – North Carolina – Guide-books. I. Title.
F252.3.B56 1989
917.5604'43 – dc20   89-32600
                                              CIP

Manufactured in the United States of America
Second Edition/Second Printing

Contents

The Piedmont *continued*

The Mountains

Introduction

I once knew a man who in his later years took to doing strange things. He would, for example, stand on his head on top of his house, often for long periods. Or he would climb atop his house, get a running start and jump off. Once, he staged his own mock hanging.

If anybody asked why he did these things, his reply was always the same.

"Just for a dadblame cur'osity," he'd say with a big grin.

Well, that's precisely why I did this book. For a dadblame cur'osity. More precisely, for a lot of them, a whole heap, as we might say in North Carolina.

In nearly twenty years of roaming around North Carolina as a newspaper reporter and columnist, I've come upon a lot of cur'osities, dadblamed and otherwise, everything from natural wonders to esoteric little museums, oddball events, private fantasy worlds, and North Carolina superlatives. Many of these things weren't widely known. They weren't in guidebooks. You couldn't pick up a travel brochure that would tell about them. No bumper stickers proclaimed them. No garish highway signs directed you to them.

It struck me that somebody ought to collect these curiosities into a guidebook so that people who have a taste for the offbeat could know about them.

Who better to do it than me, a person naturally drawn to such things?

In my travels and researches for this book, I'm sure that I didn't come upon nearly all the marvelous oddities that North Carolina has to offer. I know there must be wonders out there waiting to be discovered. If you know of any subjects worthy of inclusion in this book, I'd like to know about them for later editions. Write me at Route 6, Box 592, Asheboro, NC 27203.

The Coastal Plain

Beaufort

Aurora

Fossil Museum

All of eastern North Carolina once lay deep under the ocean, and proof of it may be seen at Aurora's Fossil Museum.

Five miles north of Aurora, Texas Gulf operates a huge phosphate mine (phosphate is an essential ingredient of fertilizer), extracting from the earth minerals left behind by long-dead marine life. Fossils as old as five million years are often found in the huge pit, and some are on display at the museum, including giant teeth from 40-foot sharks, backbones from monstrous whales, bones from long-extinct birds, and skeltons of primitve dolphins that had necks, probably proof that they were land creatures that adapted to the sea.

But fossils aren't really the focus of the museum, which tries, through murals, slide shows, a simulated phosphate pit, and other exhibits, to show how geological forces shaped the coastal area.

The museum is free. It's open Tuesday-Saturday, 10:00 A.M.-5:00 P.M. in summer, by appointment the rest of the year. For more information, call (919) 322-4111.

Bath

Remains of Blackbeard's House

America's most famous pirate, Edward Teach, otherwise known as Blackbeard, came to Bath to take his thirteenth wife. He built a house across the creek from the village in 1712.

Six years later, Blackbeard's days of plunder were brought to an end in a shipboard battle with Lt. Robert Maynard, commander of a force sent by the governor of Virginia to capture him. Maynard is said to have sailed up the Pamlico River to Bath with Blackbeard's severed head displayed on the prow of his ship.

The remains of Blackbeard's house, which can be reached only by water, are on a point across the junction of Bath and Back creeks at the end of Bath's Main Street. Many believe Blackbeard buried gold in the area, but none has been found.

Mysterious Hoofprints

In a wooded area near the town of Bath is a series of saucer-sized depressions in the earth that have mystified people for nearly 200 years. Nothing grows in the depressions, and debris placed in them will not remain.

Legend has it that the depressions were made by the hooves of a spirited horse ridden by a young man named Jesse Elliott in a race shortly after the turn of the nineteenth century. Local people frowned on Sunday horse racing, but Jesse and a group of other young men scorned them.

During one Sunday race, just after Jesse shouted, "Take me in a winner or take me to hell," his horse dug in its hooves, throwing Jesse into a nearby pine tree and killing him instantly.

The hoofprints are unmarked but regularly visited. To find them, take the Goose Creek State Park Road off US-264. The site is about a quarter mile on the left, near a pull-off created by the vehicles that stop there regularly.

North Carolina's Oldest Town and Church

Settled at the end of the seventeenth century, Bath became the first community in the American colonies to open a public library with the arrival of a shipment of religious books in 1700. In 1705, it became the first incorporated town in North Carolina. The following year, the first shipyard in the state was opened here, and the first public school soon followed. Bath became the state's first capital in 1744.

Some of the town's old buildings have been restored as a historic site and may be toured for a small fee. One building that is always open (no fee) is St. Thomas Episcopal Church, the state's oldest church, built in 1734 of brick shipped from England.

The church's treasured possessions include a 1704 Bible and candlesticks donated by King George II in 1740. The church bell, erected outside, was bought with funds given by Queen Anne and is eighteen years older than the Liberty Bell.

For some reason, Bath never prospered and grew as some early seaport towns did. Some think it was because of George Whitfield's curse. Whitfield, a celebrated Methodist evangelist, came to Bath in 1774 to save souls. The townspeople not only wouldn't listen to him; they even refused him lodging. The Reverend Whitfield let them know just what he thought of their hospitality and religious views.

"I say to the village of Bath, village you shall remain, now and forever, forgotten by men and nations until such time as it pleases God to turn the light of His countenance again upon you."

Downtown Bath was burned three times after the minister's visit, and the Reverend's curse was never forgotten.

For more information, call Bath Historic Information Center at (919) 923-3971.

House Where Edna Ferber Researched Her Most Famous Novel

The Palmer-Marsh house, built in 1744, is one of North Carolina's oldest houses. It was a rooming house when novelist Edna Ferber came to stay there in 1925, the year she won a Pulitzer Prize for her novel *So Big*. Ferber, who wrote panoramic novels about the American scene, came to research another novel.

In 1912, the James Adams Floating Theater, popularly called "The Showboat," was launched on a 128-foot-long barge in Washington, NC, and was being towed to coastal communities by a 50-foot tugboat to bring musicals and comedies to entertainment-starved people in remote areas. Ferber stayed several weeks in Bath while observing and talking with the boat's crew and cast.

The novel she wrote from her experience, *Showboat*, appeared in 1926 and became a best seller. A play adapted from the book became a classic of American musical comedy and was made into a popular movie.

The John Adams Floating Theater burned in Savannah in 1941, and Ferber died in New York in 1968. The Palmer-Marsh house is now a museum, part of the Bath Historic District and may be toured for a small fee.

Little mention is made of Ferber in Bath. She obviously didn't make a good impression. "She didn't leave a dime for the church," says local resident Ann Flanagan. "She complained about her lodging and she changed the locale of her novel to Mississippi, so she wasn't very popular here."

Belhaven

The Flea Wedding and Other Wonders
from Eva Way's Collections

Eva Way may have been the ultimate collector. Not only could Mrs. Way, a farm woman, not bear to throw anything away, she couldn't bear to see anybody else throw anything away either.

"Anybody who had anything they didn't want and didn't know what to do with, they took it to her," said her daughter, Catherine Wilkerson.

So Eva Way collected. Coins, shells, pitchers, books, magazines, newspapers, paintings, clothes, furniture, gourds, military paraphernalia, jewelry, radios, coffee mills, kitchenware, opium pipes, baskets, eyeglasses, pottery, typewriters, farm tools, and even old, everyday, worn-out shoes, which she prized above all other things. You name it, most likely Eva Way had a few, if not dozens of them.

It began with buttons when Mrs. Way was newly wed. She accummulated more than 30,000 different ones. She moved on to string from feed sacks, rolling it into huge balls. So compelling did her passion for collecting eventually become that she kept the freakish animals born on the farm, pickling them in jars and carefully labeling them ("hare-lipped puppy," "one-eyed pig"). Before it was over, she was even taking gallstones, cataracts, hideous ingrown toenails, and tumors that doctors cut from her neighbors (one monstrous pickled tumor fills a ten-gallon aquarium).

Mrs. Way packed a twelve-room house and a huge barn with her collections, and for more than forty years she kept her home open to visitors who wanted to see it all. After her death at age ninety-three in 1962, her family was perplexed about what to do with everything.

"I tried to sell it all because I was sick and tired of it," said Mrs. Wilkerson. "I sold for two years. After I got tired of selling, some ladies and I got together and decided to put it up as a museum."

The town of Belhaven accepted part of Mrs. Way's collections, and in 1965 the Belhaven Memorial Museum was opened on the second floor of the town hall.

The hit of the museum is Mrs. Way's dried flea wedding – all the fleas dressed and in church – which has to be viewed with a large magnifying glass. Nobody knows where Mrs. Way got it, but nobody was surprised that she had it.

The museum is free. It's open daily 1:00-5:00 P.M. Group tours may be arranged by calling (919) 943-4111.

Terra Ceia

Tulip Fields of Terra Ceia

In the thirties and early forties of this century, a group of Dutch immigrants settled in the flat fields of Beaufort County. Lured by the rich, black soil, they came to grow the flowers of the old country: tulips, gladiolus, irises, daffodils, hyacinths, peonies, crocuses. At one time, thirty growers raised more than 500 acres of flowers. Now only one family remains a major grower, the Staalduinens, with 200 acres, mostly tulips. Several other families still grow a few acres, and in the spring and early summer, the fields around Terra Ceia blossom beautifully. This community is on State Road 1616, off US-264, near Pantego.

Bertie

Windsor

The Largest Tree in North Carolina

A bald cypress 2¹/₂ miles northwest of Windsor on NC-308 is the largest tree in the state, judging by a point system developed by the American Forestry Association.

The tree is 138 feet tall. The trunk has a circumference of more than 38 feet. The tree has 605 points, compared to 1,010 points for the largest tree in America, the General Sherman sequoia in California. Unfortunately, North Carolina's biggest tree isn't visible from the road and can be reached only by air or a 2-mile round-trip hike through a swamp.

Bladen

Carvers

America's largest Southern Magnolia

The nation's largest southern magnolia tree is on a farm owned by
H.C. Blake at the end of State Road 1733, off NC-87, east of
Carvers. The tree stands 86 feet tall, with a crown spread of 96 feet.
The trunk has a circumference of 20 feet.

Clarkton

Whistler's Mother's Home

Part of an old brick chimney and the remains of a brick wall in a
tangle of growth are the only traces left of stately Oak Forest, the
plantation where James McNeill Whistler's mother, Anna, was
born and reared.

Anna McNeill fell in love with a West Point classmate of her
brother's, but the cadet, G.W. Whistler, married another woman.
After seven years of marriage and three children, Whistler's wife
died and he renewed his romance with Anna. They married when
she was twenty-seven, and Anna gave birth to five sons. Her
first-born, James, nicknamed Jamey, would become a painter and
make his mother famous.

After G.W. Whistler, an engineer, took a job building a railroad
in Russia, tragedy befell the family. Anna, who had followed
her husband abroad, lost him and three of her sons to illness and
returned to this country.

For a while during the Civil War, she lived at Oak Forest, but
her uneasiness at being the widow of a West Point man prompted
her to move to safety in Paris. It was there that her son James
visited her and painted her portrait. He called it *Arrangement in
Grey and Black*, but it became known as *Whistler's Mother*. Owned
by the French government, it is on permanent exhibit at the Louvre
in Paris.

Anna McNeill Whistler died in 1881 at age seventy-seven and
is buried in England. Oak Forest, built in 1737, burned in 1933.
The remains are just north of Clarkton on an unpaved road, a half
mile off State Road 1760, 1/10 of a mile from US-701.

Kelly

Oldest Tree East of the Rockies

A stand of virgin cypress trees growing along a 10-mile stretch of the Black River along the Bladen-Pender county line has been identified by a team of scientists from the University of Arkansas as containing the oldest living trees east of the Rocky Mountains. The team, which discovered the trees in 1985, found scores to be more than 1,000 years old. One tree had lived at least 1,700 years, the scientists said. Some of the trees tower more than 100 feet and have trunks 8 feet thick at the base. The North Carolina Nature Conservancy is hoping to preserve the trees, which can be seen only by canoe, although a few are visible from the NC-53 bridge.

Brunswick

Calabash

Seafood Restaurant Town

Calabash, a onetime fishing village named for an Indian word for gourds, is a town of just over 200 people with a seafood restaurant for every ten residents.

Just who opened the first restaurant in town, the Becks or Colemans, is a matter of dispute. Both families were holding outdoor oyster roasts for people from nearby communities back in the thirties. By 1940, both had moved their oyster roasts indoors and added fried seafoods.

As more customers came to eat with the Becks and Colemans, other restaurants, or fish camps, as they came to be called in North Carolina, opened in the small community, and by the sixties Calabash was drawing large crowds from nearby, ever-burgeoning Myrtle Beach.

By the seventies, Calabash had attracted national attention and Calabash-style cooking, meaning lightly battered seafood briefly fried, was being advertised by restaurants over several Southern states.

Once Calabash restaurants featured fresh seafood locally caught, but now most of it is caught elsewhere and frozen. Newer restaurants not only brought gaudy signs, bright lights, and salad bars but also fancy dishes like lobster to Calabash's simple fare, changing the whole character of Calabash.

Calabash's restaurants are lined side by side on NC-179, just off US-17, near the South Carolina line, and along a side street leading to the waterfront. Both original restaurants, Beck's and Coleman's Original Calabash, are still operated by their families. For information call Beck's at (919) 579-6776; call Original Calabash's at (919) 579-6875.

In the forties, a frequent diner at the Colemans' restaurant was entertainer Jimmy Durante. Lucy Coleman remembers that he joked with her and called her Mrs. Calabash. Durante later began closing all of his shows by saying, "Goodnight, Mrs. Calabash, wherever you are," and Lucy Coleman believes he was talking to her.

The Old Man's House

As a syndicated newspaper columnist, writer for slick magazines, and novelist, Robert Ruark enjoyed making people angry. "When people stop calling me an SOB, I'll be dead," he once said. He died at forty-nine of internal hemorrhaging while visiting London from his home in Spain.

A big-game hunter and great admirer of Ernest Hemingway, Ruark was known as a man's man. He gained his greatest fame and wealth from his best-selling books about Africa, *Something of Value* and *Uhuru*. *Something of Value*, published in 1955, so angered Kenyans that they banned him from their country. But it was a gentler book that Ruark wrote to follow that one.

The Old Man and the Boy, published in 1957, was about Ruark's boyhood experiences with his grandfather, E.H. Adkins, a Southport river pilot. Ruark, who was born in Southport, spent many happy hours in his grandfather's two-story house at 119 N. Lord Street. Built by E.H. Adkins in 1890, the house is still a private residence. It is open to visitors only occasionally on Southport home tours.

Carteret

Beaufort

Captain Sinbad's Pirate Cruises, Pirate School, and Pirate Invasion

When Ross Morphew was growing up in Ohio, the only thing he wanted to be was a pirate. When people told him that wasn't possible, he asked why. So when he grew up, he built himself a brigantine in his back yard and eventually set sail for the North Carolina waters once plied by the famous pirate Blackbeard. He outfitted his ship with cannon, flew the Jolly Roger, donned pirate garb, changed his name to Capt. Sinbad, and began attacking vessels with water balloons and occasionally spiriting away willing fair maidens.

He began taking passengers for short cruises on his ship, the *Meka II*, and in 1979 he opened the world's first pirate school, offering five-day cruising courses in such skills as burying treasure, plank walking, swinging from the yardarms, yo-ho-hoing, and swashbuckling.

Each year on the fourth weekend in April, Captain Sinbad and a band of rogues invade Beaufort and try to take it over. Each year they are beaten back by a hardy band of defenders with musketry and cannon.

For more information, call (919) 728-7213.

Strange Seafood Exhibition

Ever tried marinated octopus? How about raw squid? Live sea urchin eggs? Charcoaled shark? Mole crab soup? Smoked eel? Seaweed salad? Stingray casserole? Left-handed whelk chowder?

Thousands of people have tried such exotic fare at the North Carolina Maritime Museum's annual Strange Seafood Exhibition, held on the third Thursday of August. The event, designed to show that many strange creatures from sea and sound are not only edible but quite good (a few are pretty awful, too), features more than fifty different dishes prepared by local cooks. Demonstrations show how to gather, catch, open, clean, and prepare various creatures for eating.

This has become one of the most popular events on the North

Carolina coast, attracting national attention every year. It grew
to such a degree that crowds were no longer manageable, and now
participation is limited to 1,000 people. A fee is charged and
tickets should be ordered early.

For more information, write the North Carolina Maritime
Museum, 315 Front Street, Beaufort, NC 28516, or call (919)
728-7317.

Morehead City

Blue Crab Derby

How fast can a crab run? You can find out at the Blue Crab Derby
held each year at the Crystal Coast Civic Center on US-70 West in
Morehead City.

Races are held for both amateur and professional crab trainers,
but few professionals show up because Jean Paul Lewis, a crabber
from Smyrna and all-time champion speed crab trainer, almost
always wins all the trophies in the professional division.

In addition to the races, musical entertainment is provided along
with crab dinners. You can choose crab cakes or steamed crabs for
dinner, and don't be surprised if you think you see some of the
racers on your plate.

"We eat all the losers," says Bill Colbert, a member of the
Kiwanis Club, which sponsors the event. Call him for more information at (919) 726-2516.

Old Quawk's Day

He was a cantankerous old salt, irritable and irreligious, who
washed ashore from a shipwreck in the last century and stayed.
Other fishermen couldn't pronounce his name, so they called him
Old Quawk, because his squawking voice resembled the call of
the night heron, more commonly called the quawk.

One blustery March day when threatening skies kept other
fishermen in port, Old Quawk cursed the heavens, went to retrieve
his nets — and disappeared into legend.

Old Quawk Day is held the second Saturday in March at the
Morehead Municipal Park on US-70 West to honor the memory of
the legend.

Events include a quawk-calling contest, and Old Quawk look-alike contest, scallop skipping, and flounder flinging. Scallop skippers compete to see how many times they can make a scallop bounce on the waters of Bogue Sound. Flounder flingers see how far they can throw a slimy dead flounder.

Miserable weather is preferred for the event, but it is held even in pleasant conditions. For information, call Carteret County Chamber of Commerce at (919) 726-6831.

Bald-Headed Men of America Headquarters and Convention

Don't pretend to shield your eyes from the glare of John Capps's shiny head. Don't ask him if flies trying to land on his head skid and break their legs. They're old jokes. Call him Curly if you like, but don't expect him to laugh.

Do expect him to use a lot of lines on you.

"My philosophy is: If you haven't got it, flaunt it."

"The Lord is just, the Lord is fair, he gave some brains, the others hair."

"I'm just trying to set a shining example."

John started losing his hair at age fifteen. By twenty, he was bald. "I'm the fourth generation of baldness in my family," he says.

John Capps sets a shining example

"I grew up in a family where baldness was accepted, a way of life, so to speak. It didn't bother me at all."

But he knew it bothered a lot of other people, and that set him to thinking. In 1974, when he was thirty-three, living in Dunn, John started Bald-Headed Men of America to promote pride in baldness. It wasn't an idea that came off the top of his head. He thought about it for a long time.

The organization stirred international attention and attracted nearly 10,000 members, including celebrities such as Yul Brynner, Telly Savalas, and former President Gerald Ford. John, who became a celebrity himself, constantly in demand for appearances, moved his organization to Morehead City because he thought it a more appropriate location.

"More head, less hair," he says.

At the group's headquarters at 3819 Bridges Street, John offers Bald Is Beautiful bumper stickers and gag gifts such as toothless combs. On the second Saturday in September each year, he holds a convention at Mrs. Willis's Restaurant, where baldies compete for such titles as sexiest, smoothest, prettiest, and most kissable bald heads.

For more information, write Bald-Headed Men of America, 3819 Bridges Street, Morehead City, NC 28577, or call (919) 726-1004.

Newport

World's Largest Pig Picking

In 1979, the Newport Development Center for Children faced a crisis because of federal and state budget cuts. A group of citizens decided to hold a pig cooking contest to try to keep the center operating.

They got twenty-five sponsors, twenty-five cooks, and twenty-five pigs and hoped to sell 2,500 plates of barbecue. Days before the event, they realized they'd sold too many tickets and had to scramble to get seventeen more pigs, cooks, and sponsors.

Now a hundred pigs are cooked every year on the first weekend in April, the biggest pig-cooking contest anywhere. The competition is keen and the judging is harsh (the pigs, which are cooked all night, are judged on appearance, color, crispness of skin, doneness, taste, moisture, and sauce).

Thousands of people come to eat the results and see the entertainment, which includes music, dancing, and peripheral contests

(in 1983, a Marine choked to death before hundreds of people
during a doughnut eating contest at the event). For more information, call (919) 223-4808.

Sealevel

Snug Harbor

Capt. Richard Randall, a privateer in the early days of this nation's
history, made a lot of money from the sea and in his will, penned
by his friend Alexander Hamilton, he left money to build a home
where "aged, decrepid and worn-out seamen" could spend their
final days. He decreed that it be called Sailor's Snug Harbor.

The home was built on Staten Island in 1801 and there it
remained, overseen by trustees, until 1976, when deteriorating
buildings forced a move. Seeking a less crowded area in a milder
climate to build a new home, the trustees settled on a site on
Nelson's Bay at Sealevel, near the eastern end of US-70. More than
one hundred old mariners make their home at Sailor's Snug Harbor,
about a tenth of them female.

On the first Saturday of November, a fall bazaar is held featuring
arts and crafts made by the old salts at Snug Harbor, but visitors
are welcome any time to hear sea stories. Call (919) 225-4411.

Chowan

Edenton

America's First Political Action by Women

On October 26, 1774, fifty-one women from five eastern North
Carolina counties gathered at the home of Penelope Barker on the
courthouse green in Edenton, a town on Albemarle Sound dating
back to 1710. They drank tea and signed a document vowing
to boycott tea and other products in protest against England's high
taxes.

The document, accompanied by a letter, made its way to England where it appeared in *The Morning Chronicle & London Advertiser*
on January 6, 1775, and created a scandal because women didn't
dare involve themselves in politics at this time.

"It was the first political action by women in the American colonies," proclaims Linda Eure, director of Historic Edenton. "That's what makes it special to us."

The Edenton Tea Party, as the event came to be known, is celebrated annually on the weekend nearest the anniversary with reenactments, music, a crafts show, and other events on the Edenton waterfront. Call (919) 482-2637.

America's Largest Sand Post Oak

The largest sand post oak tree in America stands in the front yard of Herbert Wilson's house on NC-32 north of Edenton, next to the North Carolina Forest Service headquarters and fire tower. The tree is 70 feet tall with a crown spread of 79 feet. The trunk has a circumference of 11 feet.

Oldest Frame House in North Carolina

In 1972, Dr. Richard Hines, Jr., a dentist, bought an old frame house on Yeopim River that once had been in the family of his wife, Ann. The following year, he moved it to Horni Blow Point on Albemarle Sound to a lot on Bella Vista Drive, off NC-37. He added to it a den, two bedrooms, a laundry, and bath and made it into a home for his family.

Documents indicate that the house, which once was called Pine Grove and later Sycamore, may have been built in 1718, perhaps by Jacob Butler, thus making it the oldest standing frame house in North Carolina. Controversy exists about this, however. Some maintain that the Cupola House, a visitors center on Broad Street in Edenton, built around 1725, is the oldest.

Peanut Festival

Peanuts are very big in Edenton, both literally and figuratively. Some of the biggest peanuts in the world are grown near the town (it's the home of Jimbo's Jumbos), and peanuts are also the town's major industry.

Of the 15,000 acres of cropland in Chowan County, more than 6,000 are planted in peanuts, and Edenton has three major peanut processing plants. So it was only natural that the town start a Peanut Festival, which it did in 1976.

Held the first weekend in October to celebrate the harvest, the festival features a peanut parade, peanut picking demonstrations, peanut rolling races (you roll 'em with your nose), and other events. Plenty of peanuts are available for eating raw, roasted, fried, or made into peanut brittle.

Columbus

Chadbourn

Oldest Fruit Festival in the South

Chadbourn once called itself the strawberry capital of the world. From the turn of the century to the mid-thirties, strawberries were the major crop in the area.

Millions of quarts of strawberries were shipped out of Chadbourn in refrigerated railroad cars each year. Once, a million quarts were shipped in a single twenty-four-hour period. When a problem developed one year with railroad cars, tons of strawberries soured and had to be dumped in a nearby swamp. Old-timers remember that the water ran red for days.

The strawberry auction, which brought hundreds of growers and buyers to town each spring, was the highlight of the year in Chadbourn, and the Strawberry Festival, begun in 1932, grew out of it.

The auction is no more, but the festival has continued each year, making it the oldest agricultural festival in the state, and one of the oldest in the country, although soybeans and tobacco long ago replaced strawberries as area farmers' big money producers. Indeed, only a few farms grow about 125 acres of strawberries in the area now, mostly for local sale.

But Chadbourn still holds the Strawberry Festival each year on the first Friday in May out of tradition. A parade is held, along with a strawberry recipe contest. Fresh strawberries and strawberry shortcake are sold on the streets. And farmers bring their biggest and sweetest strawberries to be judged in twenty-four divisions.

The winning six-quart flats of strawberries are then sold at a charity auction. Take a lot of money if you plan to buy any. Most go for about $200 a flat, and some have brought as much as $1,200. For more information, call (919) 654-5423.

Lake Waccamaw

South's Largest Crater Lake

Lake Waccamaw, a shallow black-water lake 5 miles long and 3 miles wide, named for local Indians, is the largest of the Carolina Bays, a widely spread series of oval-shaped lakes, swamps, peat beds, and depressions in southeastern North Carolina. The bays are believed to have been caused by a meteor shower striking the earth thousands of years ago.

The lake is drained by the Waccamaw River, a beautiful, twisting stream greatly favored by canoeists. The northern edge of the lake can be reached by NC-214 from the town of Lake Waccamaw on US-74-76.

Lakes White, Bay Tree, and Singletary in Bladen County are also Carolina Bays.

Whiteville

Grave of World's Second-Most Famous Siamese Twins

On July 11, 1851, twin girls joined at the hip were born to slaves Jacob and Monemia on Jabe McCoy's plantation in the Welches Creek community northeast of Whiteville.

At that time, the original Siamese twins, Chang and Eng, who had gained worldwide fame exhibiting themselves, had settled in western North Carolina, where they married sisters and were rearing families.

McCoy was quick to realize the possibilities for his twins and sold them before they were a year old for $1,000 and 25 percent of the income from exhibiting them. But the buyer had little success showing them so young, and when they were two, McCoy waived all rights to them for $200.

The twins were sold again and by the age of four were being exhibited in Europe, where doctors determined their spines were fused, making separation impossible.

Although they had clearly separate nervous systems and minds of their own, the twins, named Millie and Christine at birth, called themselves Mille-Chrissy, thought of themselves in the singular, and frequently walked on only two of their four legs. Extraordinarily congenial, they learned to recite and sing sweetly at their exhibitions.

By age ten, the twins were back in this country, and the owner who had inherited them, Joseph Pearson Smith of South Carolina, hid them near Spartanburg during the Civil War to keep them out of the hands of Union troops.

After winning their freedom following the war, the twins, who were exceptionally bright, hired a manager and again toured Europe, where they gained great fame for their singing, learned to speak fluently in five languages, and became special favorites of England's Queen Victoria, who frequently summoned them to perform.

By the turn of the century, the twins had returned to their birthplace and built a fourteen-room house on property once owned by the man who had owned them at birth. There they frequently received friends and family and entertained on the big front porch. But in 1909 the house burned, destroying all the mementoes of their world travels.

Soon after the fire, Mille contracted tuberculosis and grew steadily weaker. She died peacefully on the afternoon of October 8, 1912, at age sixty-one, in the presence of Dr. W.H. Crowell of Whiteville, who had made acquaintance with the twins while studying in England. Chrissy, who detected her sister's death before the doctor did, lived less than a day (reports vary from eight to seventeen hours) and spent her last hours calmly praying and singing favorite hymns.

The twins were buried in a double cypress coffin in the cemetery of a small Baptist church near their home. A metal grave marker was melted in a forest fire that swept through the area years later.

In 1969, the Columbus County Historical Society got family permission to move and remark the grave. The remains were reburied in the Welches Creek Community Cemetery not far from the original site and a granite marker was erected. "A soul with two hearts," reads part of the inscription. "Two hearts that beat as one."

The Welches Creek Cemetery is on State Road 1719, off Red Hill Road, off US-74-76, east of Whiteville.

Craven

New Bern

Hall of Fame Cypress

In the walled back yard of the Samuel Smallwood Myers House
(built in 1884), a private residence, is North Carolina's most
famous tree. Thought to be more than 1,000 years old, it's one
of twenty trees in the Hall of Fame of American Trees. Early
settlers signed a peace treaty with Indians under the tree, and both
George Washington and James Monroe visited the tree. It can
be seen from a public alley beside the house by climbing onto a
car fender and peeking over the wall.

Fred the Stuffed Firehorse

Back in the days when fire engines were run by steam and pulled
by horses, Fred was one of New Bern's most dependable firehorses.
The town had two volunteer fire companies, Atlantic, organized in
1845, and Button, organized twenty years later. Fred became a fire-
horse in 1908 and pulled a hose wagon for Atlantic Company.

Fred always knew just what to do when the alarm sounded,
always responded quickly, backing into the wagon stall so the harness could be dropped over his head. He always ran hard and
seemed to take pride in getting his hose to fire scenes as quickly as
possible. He must have sensed that his working days were numbered, though, after the town got its first motorized fire wagon in
1914. Another followed a year later.

But that didn't stop Fred from giving his all. He strove to beat
the chugging trucks at every opportunity.

Fred helped fight the biggest fire that New Bern has ever seen, a
holocaust that struck in December, 1922, and nearly burned down
the town. It destroyed churches, stores, warehouses, a shipyard, and
more than 1,000 houses. A hundred buildings were dynamited to
try to stop its spread. More than 3,200 people were left homeless.

Maybe it was memories of that awful fire, or maybe it was just
the ever-growing threat from the newfangled fire engines that
caused Fred to strain ever harder at the sound of the alarm. Whatever it was, the strain proved too great.

In 1925, while racing to an alarm from box 57 at New Banks

and North streets, Fred fell dead in his harness. The alarm proved false.

Because of Fred's noble efforts, the men of Atlantic Company decided to have his head stuffed. They kept it at the fire station until 1957, when the town opened its Firemen's Museum in an old garage behind the fire station.

The museum, one of a few of its kind in the world, contains New Bern's old fire engines and wagons and a great assortment of other firefighting paraphernalia and memorabilia, but Fred's stuffed head has always been its featured attraction. The museum is now in a new building on Hancock Street, just around the corner from the fire station.

Birthplace of Pepsi-Cola

Caleb Bradham was called Doc because he liked to mix remedies in his pharmacy at the corner of Pollack and Middle streets. He made tonics for rheumatism, cramps, coughs, dandruff, constipation, and dog mange. But it wasn't until he concocted a new soft drink to sell at his marble-topped fountain that he finally hit on something that would make him rich.

All of his customers liked his new drink, which they called Brad's Drink. That gave Bradham the idea that he should turn over his drugstore to an assistant and hit the road selling the syrup he used to make his drink. He didn't particularly like calling it Brad's drink, so for $100 he bought a registered brand name, Pep Kola, from a defunct New Jersey company, and changed it to Pepsi-Cola, which he thought had more bounce. Within ten years, Bradham's drink was being sold in twenty-four states, and he was a rich man.

After World War I, problems arose. The price of sugar shot up dramatically, and fearing a shortage, Bradham invested heavily in it. Soon the market broke and the price of sugar fell to a fourth of what it had been. It broke Bradham, and his company closed. He returned to his drugstore and his remedies.

Pepsi-Cola might have disappeared completely if a few distributors hadn't stockpiled barrels of syrup. The formula for making Pepsi and the registered name had been bought from receivership, sold, and resold, before another company started making the drink in the thirties, a few years after Bradham's death.

Pepsi went on to become America's second most popular soft drink (after Coca-Cola), but Bradham's family never received any of the riches it produced.

The pharmacy where Bradham invented Pepsi is now Hearnes' Jewelry Store. A plaque on an outside wall identifies it as the birthplace of the famous drink. If he isn't busy, jeweler Richard Hearnes will take visitors to see the spot in the basement where Bradham actually mixed the first batch of syrup.

Cumberland

Fayetteville

Site of Babe Ruth's First Home Run

The year was 1914. The Baltimore Orioles had come to Fayetteville for three weeks of spring training that March because Hyman Fleishman, a transplanted Baltimorean, offered them free lodging at his Lafayette Hotel.

Joining the Orioles that year was a new player, eighteen-year-old George Herman Ruth. Because he was cherub-faced and the youngest member of the team, the other players started calling him Babe.

During an intra-squad game at the old Cape Fear Fairgrounds off Gillespie Street, "the babe" hit a ball 405 feet out of the park, across a corn field and into a lake, his first, unofficial home run as a professional player. He later would go on to hit 714 official home runs in his career, a record broken only by Hank Aaron.

The ballpark is gone now. A State Highway Department office occupies the site. But a historic marker has been erected by the state, thanks to a three-year campaign by Maurice Fleishman, son of Hyman, who as a bat boy for the Orioles saw Babe hit that first home run.

House Where Carson McCullers Wrote Her First Novel

Carson McCullers, a Georgia native who became one of the South's most highly acclaimed writers, lived with her husband, Reeves, on the second floor of Cool Spring Tavern at 119 Cool Spring Street from 1938 to 1940, while she was finishing her first novel, *The Heart Is a Lonely Hunter*.

The couple moved to Fayetteville because Reeves was transferred there by the loan company he worked for, and they disliked the town intensely. McCullers' book was published to rave reviews in 1940, and the couple used the first royalties to move to New York. A Peeping Tom incident that occurred at Ft. Bragg while McCullers was living in Fayetteville inspired her second novel, *Reflections in a Golden Eye.*

Tenth Hole of Original Putt Putt

Don Clayton, a former quarterback at the University of North Carolina, was a hotshot insurance agent in his home town, making a lot of money and sometimes working twenty hours a day, when he realized something was wrong. His doctor told him he was about to have a nervous breakdown and advised him to take a month off.

During that month, Don played a round of miniature golf at a crude course and was struck by the idea that the game would be more fun on a better designed, more challenging course. So he sat down and designed one he thought would be better. He built it for $2,500 on leased land on Bragg Boulevard at a junction called the Crossover, and opened it on June 21, 1954.

He was planning to call the place Shady Vale Miniature Golf Course, but when he went to open an account at the bank, he realized he wasn't sure how to spell Vale and began trying to think of another name.

"I said, 'Well, it's putting,' " he recalls, "'and what rhymes with putt?' There wasn't anything, so I called it Putt Putt."

His golf course was an immediate success and by that fall he had already started building others in other cities. There are now more than 1,400 Putt Putts around the world, all of them using the holes, green carpets, and orange rails designed by Don.

The original Putt Putt is gone. The lease on the land expired after fourteen years and Don built a new fifty-four-hole course two blocks west on Bragg Boulevard. But the concrete part of the tenth hole of the original course still exists behind the One-Hour Koretizing Dry Cleaners and Kasey's Restaurant.

The International Firefighters Museum

Even as a small child, Chris Fischer was fascinated by fire trucks and determined to become a fireman. At sixteen he volunteered to wash trucks and mop floors at a neighborhood fire station. By the age of eighteen, he was a fireman, but five years later his dream job was eliminated by a cut in federal funds.

Determined to remain in firefighting, Chris established the Children's Fire Museum in 1983 and began presenting programs on firefighting at schools and shopping malls. By 1986, he had reorganized the Children's Fire Museum into the International Firefighters Museum.

The museum now occupies a back room of Chris's house at 722 Tupelo Circle off the Raeford Road. It features more than 1,000 articles of firefighting paraphernalia from every state and several foreign countries.

Chris hopes the museum eventually will be located in a fire house and that it will feature items from every country and tell the story of firefighting worldwide.

Each year on the first weekend in June, Chris holds a ceremony to honor fallen firefighters, recognize fire departments for heroic deeds, and induct new members into his Firefighters Hall of Fame. The museum may be seen by appointment. Call (919) 425-5083.

Ft. Bragg

War Museums

Ft. Bragg, one of the largest military bases in the United States, home of the Eighty-second Airborne, the First Special Operations Command, and the Eighteenth Airborne Corps, the country's premier ready force, is an open post allowing free access to visitors.

Parachute drops are made almost daily at the sprawling post, and visitors are invited to watch. Time of the jumps and locations of drop zones are recorded daily on tapes at the visitors center at the Main Post Parade Field on Randolph Street.

Two more interesting spots for vistors are the Eighty-second Airborne Division Museum and the Special Forces Museum. At the first, the story of the Eighty-second is told in a slide show, and a large amount of memorabilia, especially from World War II, including captured weapons and materiel, airplanes that para-troopers jumped from, and a mock-up of a World War II glider, may be seen.

Weapons and paraphernalia from the Vietnam War may be seen at John F. Kennedy Special Warfare Museum.

Both museums are on Ardennes Road, about three miles apart. The Eighty-second Airborne Division Museum, on the corner of Ardennes and Gela streets in Building C-6841, is open Tuesday-

Saturday, 10:00 A.M.-4:30 P.M.; Sunday 11:30 A.M.-4:00 P.M. Closed Mondays, except on legal holidays; then open 10:00 A.M.-4:30 P.M. For information, call (919) 432-5307.

The John F. Kennedy Special Warfare Museum, located in Building D-2502 on the corner of Ardennes and Marion streets, is open Tuesday-Sunday, 11:30 A.M.-4:00 P.M., but not on most legal holidays. For information, call (919) 432-1533.

Dare

Buxton

Tallest Lighthouse in the United States

Cape Hatteras Lighthouse, built of brick in 1870, is 208 feet tall, making it the tallest lighthouse in the United States. Its automatic light, warning ships off the most treacherous waters of the Atlantic Coast, can be seen 51 miles offshore.

The lighthouse is threatened by the ever-encroaching surf, and a campaign has been started to raise money to keep it from being claimed by the waters it warns against.

The lighthouse, just south of Buxton, off NC-12, is maintained by the National Park Service.

Hatteras Lighthouse, tallest in the United States

Hatteras

First National Seashore

In 1833, Frank Stick, an artist, wrote an article suggesting that
much of North Carolina's Outer Banks – fragile, largely wild
barrier islands that he had chosen for his home – should be
preserved as a coastal park. The idea caught on and such a park
was authorized by Congress in 1937.

World War II intervened before the park could be established,
however, and for a while the plan seemed dead. But it was revived
after the war and land acquisition began. Dedicated finally in 1958,
Cape Hatteras National Seashore became the first park of its kind.

The park includes the southern part of Bodie Island and most of
Hatteras and Ocracoke Islands, excluding the villages of Rodanthe,
Waves, Salvo, Avon, Buston, Frisco, Hatteras, and Ocracoke. It
offers visitors nearly 70 miles of primitive beach along with visitor
centers and camping areas. NC-12 traverses the park.

Kill Devil Hills

Site of Man's First Powered Flight

The Wright brothers, Wilber and Orville, bicycle shop owners and
tinkerers from Dayton, Ohio, first became interested in the idea
of manned flight near the end of the nineteenth century. In 1900,
when Wilber was thirty-three and Orville twenty-nine, they built
a glider and began looking for a place with appropriate winds to
test it.

They chose the windswept sand dunes of North Carolina's Outer
Banks, and in the fall of that year, they set up camp near Kill Devil
Hills and began their experiments. They returned each fall for the
next two years with new gliders and broke all records for glider
experiments at that time: largest flown, longest in the air, smallest
angle of descent, flight in highest wind. They also built the first
wind tunnel to use in their experiments.

Those experiments convinced them that a motor-powered
manned craft could fly, and in 1903 they built such a craft and
returned to Kill Devil Hills with it that fall. They suffered many
problems and frustrations, causing them to stay longer than usual.
But on December 14, with Wilber at the controls, their spindly
craft almost cleared the wooden launching ramp before it stalled.

Site of man's first powered flight, the Wright Brothers Memorial.

They were certain it would fly, however, and after a day of repairs to the machine and another day of waiting for the right winds, they made another attempt. At 10:30 A.M., December 17, their plane carried Orville aloft for twelve seconds, a distance of 100 feet, man's first flight in a powered craft. They took turns flying it three more times that morning. The last flight carried Wilber 852 feet in fifty-seven seconds. Soon after the flights, a gust of wind caught the unanchored plane and flipped it end over end, wrecking it.

The Wright Brothers National Memorial, an imposing granite structure on a dune overlooking the site of the first flight, is on the US-158 bypass at milepost 7. The visitors' center and museum contains a full-scale model of the Wrights' first plane. Their camp and the wooden runway have been reconstructed at the original site. The memorial is open daily, 8:00 A.M.-6:30 P.M. in summer, 8:30 A.M.-4:30 P.M. the rest of the year. For information, call (919) 441-7430.

Each year on the first weekend in May a fly-in is held at the memorial, attracting more than 300 planes, some among the rarest and most unusual on earth.

Man Will Never Fly Memorial Society Dinner

The Man Will Never Fly Memorial Society was organized in 1959 to counter the annual observance of Wilber and Orville Wright's first flight of a powered craft on the dunes of Kill Devil Hills on December 17, 1903.

The society believes that the first flight was faked and as a result a massive fraud is being perpetuated.

"The society contends that deep down inside we all know that no machine made of tons of metal is going to 'fly,'" the society says.

But because of the Wright brothers, "people have been soaring into – and plummeting from – the skies ever since because they believe it can be done. We contend that is faith – faith misplaced and resulting from a deliberate fraud.

"How many unexplained air crashes are there and in how many of these did the pilot say to himself, 'Son of a gun – the Man Will Never Fly Memorial Society is right. This thing can't possibly fly'? Crash. More headlines."

The society's slogan is "Birds fly – men drink." Its pledge is: "Given a choice we will never fly: given no choice we will never fly sober." The society numbers 5,000 members. Membership is $2 for a lifetime. Each year on December 16, the society holds a dinner to present awards for dubious achievements in aviation. For more information, write the society at P.O. Box 1903, Kill Devil Hills, NC 27948.

Kitty Hawk

World's Highest Flying Kites

The most modern, fastest, and highest-flying kites on earth can be seen at the Rogallo Kite Festival each year on the first weekend in June. The events include kite-making workshops, kite-flying competitions, exhibits of rare and unusual kites, and a kite auction. Awards are presented by Francis Rogallo, kite designer and inventor of the hang glider. The festival is at Jockey's Ridge State Park on US-158. Call (919) 441-4124.

Manteo

America's Oldest Symphonic Outdoor Drama

The Lost Colony, the story of the mysterious disappearance of the first English settlement in the New World, became America's first symphonic outdoor drama when it opened July 4, 1937. President Franklin D. Roosevelt came to see the show the following month.

The drama, which by the end of the 1983 season had won an audience of nearly 2.5 million since its opening, was written by North Carolina playwright Paul Green, who won a Pulitzer Prize in 1927 for his first play, *In Abraham's Bosom*. Green, who wrote several Broadway hits and movies, became known as the father of outdoor drama and wrote several others after *The Lost Colony*.

The drama has been presented every year since 1937, except for two years during World War II when the coast was blacked out, at the Waterside Theater at Ft. Raleigh National Historic Site on Roanoke Island, where the first English settlement was attempted.

An important moment in Paul Green's The Lost Colony – *the first outdoor drama of its kind – is this scene set in Plymouth, England. Here, Sir Walter Raleigh bids farewell to the brave band of settlers who are about to sail for their new home in what would eventually become North Carolina. The epic drama has been staged by veteran Broadway/ Hollywood director Joe Layton. It is presented on the spot where the colony settled and vanished, Roanoke Island on the Outer Banks. Photo: J. Foster Scott*

The site is off US-64. The play is presented nightly except Sunday at 8:30 P.M. from June 15 through September 1.

Andy Griffith, who has a home in Manteo, played Sir Walter Raleigh in the drama before going on to stardom and still attends at least one performance every year. Joe Layton, multiple-award-winning director and choreographer, with many Broadway and movie successes to his credit, directed and choreographed *The Lost Colony* for many years.

For more information, call The Lost Colony box office, open June through August, at (919) 473-3414; or the business office, open year round, at (919) 473-2127.

The Nation's Oldest Grapevine

The country's original wine is believed to have been made from the sweet golden scuppernong grapes of an ancient vine. Some contend that this Mother Vine was planted by the first English settlers in America, from the famed Lost Colony. Others say the vine, which still bears fruit, is at least 300 years old. Records show that the vine was old in the 1750s. A vineyard and small winery were developed around the vine earlier in this century, but the area is now an exclusive housing development.

The gnarled and twisted vine is on private property just east of Manteo on Mother Vineyard Road off US-64. The vine is on the left about 300 feet past where the road takes a sharp turn at the bay.

Oldest Working U. S. Tugboat

If there is an older working tugboat in the country than the *Lookout*, Harry Schiffman hasn't been able to find it. Harry, who operates the Salty Dog Marina on a creek behind Manteo Middle School, found the tug in the swampy headwaters of the Alligator River in 1981. The boat, which had been used to push log barges, had been out of service a couple of years. The company that owned it was bankrupt.

The *Lookout*, Harry discovered, had been built of cold steel in Camden, NJ, in 1862, equipped with a steam engine and used to haul ammunition to Yankee soldiers during the Civil War.

Harry rebuilt the 61-foot boat, which long ago had had its steam engine replaced with a diesel engine, and is now using it to haul

The Lookout, oldest tug in America.
Photo: J. Foster Scott

road building materials from the mainland to the Outer Banks.
When it's not tugging or pushing, the old boat can be seen at Salty
Dog Marina.

Andy Griffith's Tree Farm

Andy Griffith, who was born in Mt. Airy, was a high school
English teacher in Goldsboro. He appeared in *The Lost Colony*
outdoor drama in summer and frequently did comedy routines for
civic groups, when he cut a comedy record called "What It Was
Was Football," recorded at an insurance company dinner in
Greensboro.

The record sold more than a million copies, got Andy appearances in major night clubs, and led to his first big movie role in
No Time for Sergeants.

Although he has appeared in numerous movies and TV shows,
Andy's biggest success came in the long-running "Andy Griffith
Show," a television classic in which he played Sheriff Andy Taylor
of fictional Mayberry, North Carolina. The show, still tops in
reruns, has spawned many fan clubs and several books.

Soon after Andy achieved financial success, he bought a house
and 57 acres on Roanoke Sound. There he started a tree farm and

now makes it his summer home. The modest house is visible from the water but not from a public road. Andy's trees, however, are visible alongside US-64, about three-fourths of a mile south of the Airport Road, north of Manteo. Visitors are not received.

Alexander Midgett's Whale

Until 1928, when the county built a toll bridge connecting Roanoke Island to Bodie Island, no cars prowled the Outer Banks.

As soon as the bridge was completed, a Banker named Alexander Midgett saw opportunity. He opened the first gas station on the Outer Banks on the beach near the bridge.

In 1930, a year before the first stretch of highway was built on the Outer Banks, a huge blue whale, 72 feet long, washed onto the beach near Midgett's store, and he dragged it from the water with his Model T Ford. When the great whale's flesh had decayed, Midgett mounted the skeleton on a scaffold in front of his place, not only creating the first tourist attraction on the Outer Banks but giving the spot a name: Whalebone Junction.

Alexander Midgett died in 1935, but his wife, Neva, called Mama Midgett by Outer Banks visitors, kept the store and service station operating until it burned in 1941. Vandals carried away most of the bones of Alexander Midgett's whale, but Mama Midgett salvaged a 15-foot jawbone and several sections of back-bone and exhibited them in the yard of a tourist home she later operated in Manteo.

Those bones are now on display at the North Carolina Aquariums just off US-64, west of Manteo. The aquariums, which offer free exhibits and programs about marine life, are open 9:00 A.M.-5:00 P.M., Monday-Saturday, and 1:00-5:00 P.M., Sunday.

Elizabeth II

When North Carolina celebrated the 400th anniversary of the arrival of English explorers and settlers on its shores, the center-piece of the festivities was a 68-foot, three-masted bark, a replica of the ships that had brought those daring souls to a primitive land.

The ship, built of juniper and pine with $670,000 in private donations, was launched in November 1983 and completed the following spring. It is permanently docked at a visitor center on Ice Plant Island, across from downtown Manteo, except when it sails to other coastal towns for special events. Crew members in period dress show visitors around the vessel, answering questions in Old English dialect.

The ship and visitor center-museum are open 10:00 A.M.-6:00 P.M. daily from late April until November 1, and 10:00 A.M.-4:00 P.M. Tuesday-Sunday the remainder of the year. Admission is charged.

Nags Head

Ghost Ship

Residents of the Outer Banks awoke on the morning of January 31, 1921, to see a beautiful five-masted sailing vessel aground on a sandbar at treacherous Diamond Shoals, where many ships had met their end.

Strangely, no distress signals were flying from the ship, but two lifesaving crews struck out for the ship anyway to remove the crew. Seas proved too heavy for them to reach the ship, and they had to turn back. They did get close enough to see the ship's name, *Carroll A. Deering*, but they were surprised that no crew members were to be seen on deck.

Lifesavers finally reached the ship next morning to find no crew at all, only a cat. Food had been cooked and the table prepared for the crew's meal, but nobody had eaten. Nothing seemed amiss, except for a missing lifeboat and some disorder among the captain's maps.

The crew was never found and no bodies ever washed ashore. Several weeks after the ship ran aground, it was dynamited as a hazard to navigation, but residents of the Outer Banks still talk about the mystery of the ghost ship.

In 1982, Melvin Kooker, owner of a commercial haunted house in Virginia Beach, built a landlocked model of the *Carroll A. Deering* at milepost 16 on the US-158 bypass at Nags Head and opened it as "The Ghost Ship."

The five-masted triple-decked model, 110 feet long, provides the setting for the retelling of the story of the *Deering* with live actors to visitors who are guided through the ship. It is open Memorial Day to Labor Day for a fee.

Lynanne Westcott's windmill

Lynanne Westcott's Windmill

At one time more than 200 windmills whirled on the Outer Banks, grinding grain for settlers, but all of them disappeared.

Lynanne Westcott saw a picture of one of them while browsing through a history book and was so taken with its beauty that she embarked on a year's research of Outer Banks windmills. At the end of that year, she decided to build one of her own.

She chose the old mill that once stood at Buxton as her model, and four years later she finished her replica of it. It was 35 feet tall with a grinding house 9 feet by 12. Its four blades, 15 feet long and 6 feet wide, were covered with linen sailcloth.

Lynanne got the windmill operating in November, 1981, and it became the only commercial grain-grinding windmill in America. But in July 1982, Lynanne was transferred to Philadelphia by the National Parks Service and that fall she had to sell her property on the Outer Banks, including – reluctantly – her windmill.

The new owners closed the windmill and it later became part of a restaurant just off the US-158 bypass.

America's Highest Sand Dune

Jockey's Ridge, a towering sand dune just off the US-158 bypass, is a freak of nature created by man's meddling with the environment. Early settlers on the Outer Banks, as North Carolina's fragile barrier islands are called, cut trees and allowed stock to overgraze. Wind erosion began shifting the exposed sands, and the huge dune built up gradually until it was more than 100 feet tall. At times the dune, which is continually moving westward, is as tall as 125 feet.

The dune provides a magnificent view of island, sound, and sea and has been a tourist attraction since the nineteenth century. Legend once held that the woman who accompanied a man to its summit would soon become his wife.

In the early seventies, local residents became alarmed by development near the dune, and the property was purchased and made into a state park in 1975.

Hang gliders regularly provide a colorful spectacle at the dune, and each year in May, the Hang Gliding Spectacular, a three-day competition, is held. Hang gliding enthusiasts occasionally have the opportunity to meet the man who made their sport possible. Francis Rogallo, who invented the hang glider while

Hang gliding off America's highest sand dune
Photo: Kitty Hawk Kites

doing research on space capsule re-entry for NASA, lives nearby
and frequently visits the dune. For more information on the Hang
Gliding Spectacular, call (919) 441-4124.

Rodanthe

Old Christmas

Outer Bankers have always been independent and Old Christmas is
evidence of that.

When King George II ordered England and its colonies to
switch from the Julian to the Gregorian calendar in 1752, which
meant a loss of eleven days, Outer Bankers rebelled and continued
to celebrate Christmas on the old day, which that year fell on
January 5.

The tradition has continued. Now Old Christmas is celebrated
on the Saturday closest to January 5 (so long as it doesn't fall on

New Year's weekend), with a shooting match, oyster roast, chicken stew, and square dance at the Rodanthe Community Center.

Highlight of the occasion is the traditional appearance of Ol' Buck, a mythical maverick steer that could never be found during open-range roundups. "Be good," generations of Outer Banks children have been told, "or Ol' Buck will get you." Buck shows up once a year just as a reminder.

In years past, Old Christmas celebrations were a bit rowdy. "There used to be more fighting," one resident remembers. "They would fight until the last man would fall."

Salvo

The Second-Smallest Post Office in America

The Salvo Post Office on NC-12 attracts a lot of attention. A frame building 8 feet by 12, it was built shortly after the turn of the century and has been in continuous service since. It contains boxes for ninety-four patrons and sitting room for postmaster Edward Hooper, a Salvo native born in 1922.

Many travelers think it must be the smallest post office in America and stop to find out. It isn't.

The post office in Ochopee, Florida, in the Everglades is only

Postmaster Edward Hooper and America's second-smallest post office

7 feet by 8, leaving Salvo second in smallness. That doesn't keep people from taking snapshots of it, though. "I have my picture made so much I feel like a model," says Hooper.

Duplin

Kenansville

The House Where Henry Flagler Married

Liberty Hall, a plantation house, was built in 1830 by Thomas Kenan II, a member of one of North Carolina's most prominent early families. By the turn of the century, the house had passed to Mary Lily Kenan, a friend of Henry Flagler, onetime partner of John D. Rockefeller, railroad owner, and developer of South Florida.

In 1901, Flagler, then seventy-one and twice married, asked Mary Lily, then thirty-four, to marry him, and Liberty Hall became the site of North Carolina's most famous wedding.

Legend has it that Flagler built a railroad spur to Kenansville in order to whisk away his bride in his private railroad car. He built Mary Lily a marble palace in Palm Beach, and she went there to live, leaving Liberty Hall to fall into disrepair.

The house has since been restored and may be toured for a small fee. Mary Lily's wedding dress is on display. The house is on NC-24 in Kenansville and is open Tuesday-Saturday, 10:00 A.M.-4:00 P.M., and on Sunday, 2:00-4:00 P.M. For more information, call (919) 296-0522.

Rose Hill

Native Wine

Before the Civil War, North Carolina was the nation's leading wine-making state. The 1840 census showed more than 6,000 acres of vineyards in the state, with thirty-three wineries producing more than a million gallons of wine, primarily from native muscadine grapes.

The Civil War ended wine production in the state, and although it revived later, Prohibition knocked it for another loop in the twenties. But interest in wine production began to revive again in the sixties, and now the state boasts three wineries – one at Biltmore House in Asheville, bottling estate wines, a tiny one at Germantown near Winston-Salem, and by far the biggest, the Duplin Wine Cellars in Rose Hill.

David Fussell, a former high school principal and part-time grape grower, started Duplin Wine Cellars as a farmers' co-op in 1972, and its first wines went to market in 1976. The winery makes wines ranging from sweet to dry using native grapes, and even makes a North Carolina champagne from a 200-year-old recipe.

World's Largest Frying Pan

Dennis Ramsey, owner of a feed company in Rose Hill, was visiting poultry producers in Maryland when he saw what was claimed to be the world's largest frying pan. It was about 10 feet in diameter, and local poultry producers used it for big chicken frys.

Ramsey decided that Rose Hill, another poultry center, should have a bigger pan for the annual North Carolina Poultry Producers Jubilee, which had just begun in the town. He instructed one of his employees to build it.

Clarence Brown remembers working on the pan with a couple of other employees off and on for about six months. They built it of quarter-inch steel with eight pie-shaped wedges so that it would be portable. They made it 15 feet in diameter, 6 inches deep, and added a 7-foot handle.

Forty gas burners are required to fire the pan, which is capable of frying more than 250 chickens at once.

The pan is now permanently mounted under a shelter in Little League Park on Sycamore Street (US-117). It is used for frying chicken during Rose Hill's Fall Jamboree, held around the first weekend in October, which replaced the Poultry Jubilee in 1983.

Edgecombe

Princeville

First U.S. Black Town

Soon after the Emancipation Proclamation, a small group of freed slaves settled on land across the Tar River from the colonial town of Tarboro. They called their community Freedom Hill, but the name was changed to Princeville, in honor of a community leader, Turner Prince, when the community incorporated in 1885, becoming the first black town in the United States.

The town was poor, with many of its residents living in shanties and working on nearby farms or in Tarboro homes for subsistence pay. Princeville was devastated by floods until town fathers began a twenty-five-year campaign that in 1967 resulted in the construction of a dike that has since prevented more flooding.

Although the town still has no business district or industry and has only one traffic light, it has seen many improvements in recent years. Most of the town's shanties have been replaced by subsidized apartment complexes. Streets have been paved, sidewalks built, and water and sewer systems installed. Population has grown to some 2,300, but it remains 90 percent black.

Rocky Mount

World's Oldest Hardee's

In 1960, soon after North Carolina's first McDonald's opened on Summit Avenue in Greensboro, Wilber Hardee drove from his home in Greenville to have a look at this new fast-service hamburger place that he'd been hearing so much about. So impressed was he that he returned home and built himself a hamburger stand almost identical to the red-and-white tile building with walk-up windows that he had seen in Greensboro.

He called his place Hardee's, and the big difference between it and the McDonald's in Greensboro was that his place had big red Hs instead of golden arches. Like McDonald's, he sold fifteen-cent hamburgers, french fries, and milkshakes, and his location on Fourteenth Street near the campus of East Carolina University brought him lots of customers.

Business was so good that it attracted the attention of an accountant in Rocky Mount named Leonard Rawls and a budding young business-man, Jim Gardner, who later became a congress-man and lieutenant governor. They talked Wilber into joining them in a corporation to create a chain of hamburger stands to be called Hardee's. Shortly after they opened the second Hardee's on Church Street at the intersection of Falls Road in Rocky Mount, Wilber became disillusioned because he was always outvoted by his partners and had no real say in company decisions. He sold out to them for $20,000.

Wilber went on to open numerous other restaurants, most of which failed. He still operates restaurants in Greenville.

Hardee's flourished and is now the world's third-biggest ham-burger chain (after McDonald's and Burger King), with 3,100 restaurants and sales of over $3 billion a year. The company's six-story headquarters is on US-64. The first restaurant opened by the chain still operates as a company showpiece in its original design on Church Street. The original Hardee's building in Greenville has been remodeled into a medical clinic.

Gates

Gatesville

Virgin Cypress

A stand of two dozen virgin cypress trees remains in Lassiter Swamp 5 miles up Bennetts Creek from Merchants Millpond State Park, about 6 miles east of Gatesville, off US-158. Nobody knows for sure, but the trees are believed to be more than 1,000 years old, and some may have been standing in the time of Christ. The trees may be seen by canoe, which can be rented at the park.

Halifax

Hollister

Haliwa-Saponi Powwow

The Haliwa Indians, a group of about 2,500 people who took their
name from the counties in which they live, Halifax and Warren,
trace their ancestry to the Saponi Indians who once lived in eastern
North Carolina. But until 1965, when the state finally recognized
them as one of five different Indian tribes in the state, they had
trouble convincing people of their heritage.

Since that time, they have held a celebration every year on the
third weekend in April to celebrate their recognition. A campfire
is held on Friday night and on Saturday comes the crowning of the
Haliwa-Saponi princess, native dances, and demonstrations of
beadwork and basketry.

A highly acclaimed treat at the event is the traditional fry bread,
served with honey.

For more information, call (919) 586-4017.

Harnett

Angier

Tink Coats's Bell Tower and Museum

Robert Floyd Coats, a long-time high school principal in Harnett
County, was called Tink because he loved to tinker with all sorts of
things. Gadgets fascinated him and so did old tools and other
instruments. But nothing fascinated him more than bells. During
his lifetime, he collected dozens of bells, from little tinklers to
big bongers 4 feet across.

A bell isn't much good if it can't be rung, and Tink wanted to
ring his. So in 1968, at age eighty-one, Tink decided to build
himself a bell tower in his front yard. It took him three years
and when he finished he had a magnificent tower built of steel, 55
feet tall with a base 15 feet by 20, anchored in concrete 12 feet
deep. From the tower hung thirty-two bells, ranging from 1 foot
in width to nearly 5 feet. From each hung a rope, and Tink could

ring his bells to his heart's content.

In 1972, Tink completed a building next to his house for his antiques museum, and it became a community gathering spot. Each year until his death in 1976 at age eighty-five, Tink held community bell ringings on Easter, Independence Day, and New Year's Eve.

Tink's great-nephew, Tim Penny, who now lives in his house, continues the tradition, and he and his wife, Vicki, keep Tink's museum open to visitors on weekends and special occasions. Tim, an avid fan of the University of North Carolina football team, has begun his own tradition of ringing the bells after every Carolina touchdown.

The bell tower is on State Road 1309, .8 of a mile off NC-210, 6 miles southeast of Angier. To see the museum by special appointment, call Tim at (919) 894-4532.

Bunnlevel

Chief Little Beaver's Hattadare Village

On three different nights after he turned off his television, James Lowery saw on the screen the image of a man he believes to be his great-grandfather, Henry Berry Lowery, a legendary hero of the Lumbee Indians. He took the vision as a sign that he should do something to bring honor to his people. Thus he formed the Hattadare Nation, decreed himself Chief Little Beaver, and began building the Hattadare Indian Village Historical Park around his trailer on the side of US-401.

Like many Indians of eastern North Carolina, Little Beaver believes that the first English settlement in this country, which came to be known as the Lost Colony, wasn't really lost but instead intermarried with the Hatteras Indians who had welcomed the first English explorers and moved inland from Roanoke Island. He named his nation for the Hatteras Indians and for Virginia Dare, the first English child born in this country, whom Little Beaver calls the mother of his tribe. He erected a statue of Virginia Dare in his park, along with one of Henry Berry Lowery. He also built teepees, a waterfall, a covered wagon, concrete cacti, and a model of the thirteen-story pyramid he hopes eventually to build as a temple for his people. Little Beaver, who favors Western attire, receives visitors at no charge.

Dunn

The General Lee Museum

No, this isn't the General Lee so commonly honored throughout the South. This is General Bill Lee, a local boy who as a U.S. Army major conceived and planned this country's first airborne fighting force just before World War II. Major Lee soon became Major General Lee, commander of the 101st Airborne Division, which played a crucial role in this country's victory over Germany.

Soon after planning the Airborne's role in the Normandy invasion, General Lee suffered a heart attack that forced him into retirement, but during the invasion, as his troops jumped from their planes, they shouted, "Bill Lee~~!" in his honor.

General Lee returned to his hometown to the three-story brick house at 209 West Divine Street that he'd bought ten years earlier, and there he died in 1948 at age fifty-three.

In 1986, townspeople restored the house and opened it as a museum. The first floor remains as it was when General Lee lived there. Exhibits on the second floor tell the story of the Airborne. The third floor houses General Lee's personal memorabilia. The museum is open Tuesday-Friday, 10:00 A.M-4:00 P.M., Saturday, 11:00 A.M.-4:00 P.M., and Sunday, 1:00-4:00 P.M. An admission charge is being considered. A statue of General Lee stands in front of the city hall on Broad Street.

Erwin

World's Largest and Smallest Pairs of Blue Jeans

The town of Erwin grew around a cotton mill that produced denim for the overalls of eastern North Carolina farmers. That plant, now part of Burlington Industries, has become the world's largest producer of denim and the primary employer in Erwin. To acknowledge that, Erwin holds a Denim Days celebration each year on the second weekend in October.

If you don't wear jeans or some other form of denim on Denim Days, you can be locked up in a mock jail.

To help celebrate, there are beauty pageants, a rodeo, a fishing contest, a water ski show, a craft show, sky-diving exhibitions, and contests to pick the best designers and makers of denim outfits.

In front of the denim plant on Burlington Avenue, the world's largest roll of denim, more than 6 feet tall and 5 feet wide, is displayed along with the world's largest and smallest pairs of jeans. The largest jeans have a 72-inch waist and are more than 10 feet long. The smallest have only a 2-inch waist, appropriate for a small doll.

For more information, call (919) 897-7300.

Hoke

Raeford

Turkey Olympics

No state processes more turkeys for market than North Carolina, and no town processes more than Raeford. Thus, each year, on the third weekend in September, Raeford celebrates the breastbone, so to speak, of its economy with the Turkey Festival. Turkey dishes are served. A crafts show is held in which almost every item that can be made in the shape of a turkey is sold. But the highlight of the festival is the Turkey Olympics, an event featuring turkey races and a turkey dress-up contest. Winners of the events receive – what else? – frozen turkeys. Call (919) 875-5929.

Hyde

Ocracoke

Wild Banker Ponies

At one time more than 1,000 small wild horses roamed Ocracoke Island and Cape Hatteras. How they came to be there is a mystery. Some believe the horses were descended from stock brought by the first colonists. Others think they came from Spanish shipwrecks, a more likely explanation, since scientific tests have proved that the russet-colored horses came from Spanish mustangs. Formerly, the horses were regularly rounded up and sold. Now fewer than two dozen remain and they are kept penned by the National Park Service on the west side of NC-12 between the Hatteras Ferry and Ocracoke village.

East's Biggest Sand Sculpture Contest

Sand castles are always washed away by the next tide, but that doesn't keep them from being built by the scores during the annual Ocracoke Island Sand Sculpture Contest held each July 4.

The event, sponsored by the National Park Service and the Ocracoke Civic Club, grows bigger each year. In recent years it has attracted some 1,500 participants, who joined to create not only elaborate sand castles but whole villages and sea monsters.

One winner sculpted a family sunbathing on the beach. A group of college students dug a huge hole in the sand and sculpted three sets of feet at the bottom. They called it "Six Feet Deep." Call (919) 995-5209.

Johnston

Benson

America's Largest and Oldest Gospel Singing

Back in 1921, five of Benson's most prominent business and civic leaders got to talking about how much they loved gospel music and decided they'd just have a big singing at a tobacco warehouse.

They had such a good time that they decided to make it an annual event. It grew so popular that the family that founded Benson deeded the town a complete downtown block to be called the Singing Grove to provide a place for the annual event, which came to be called the North Carolina State Singing Convention.

The free event, held every year since 1921, is on the weekend of the fourth Sunday in June. It is now a two-day event, beginning at 2:00 P.M. Saturday and continuing through Sunday afternoon.

More than a hundred groups of singers appear every year to compete for trophies and more than 50,000 people turn out to hear them.

"Some of the groups kind of modernize it a little bit," says P.B. Wood, president of the association that stages the singing, "but mostly it's just good ol' Southern gospel."

Mule Day

In 1950, when Benson first held Mule Day, mule teams could still be seen working in the vast flat farmlands surrounding the town. Folks in town wanted to do something to honor these faithful workers, so they staged Mule Day, and farmers from several counties came with their mules. Hundreds of mules paraded through the streets and competed in contests.

But as the years passed, mules disappeared from the fields and fewer showed up for Mule Day. Then in the mid-1970s came a turnaround. Mules were rediscovered. People started raising them for fun, to pull wagon trains and take to special events. Now more than 1,000 mules show up in Benson on the last Saturday in September to parade and compete in beauty contests, pulling events, and races. Hundreds of horses show up, too.

In addition to the mule events, there are a rodeo and a street dance. Dancers are advised to watch their step.

Smithfield

Ava Gardner Museum

When Tom Banks was ten, growing up in Wilson, playing on the campus of Atlantic Christian College, he used to banter with a pretty student who waited each day for a ride near the spot where he played. He couldn't have imagined then that one day that bantering would result in one of North Carolina's more unusual museums.

Tom didn't learn the pretty girl's name until some time after she had disappeared from the campus. Then he saw her picture in the newspaper one day with the startling revelation that she was marrying movie star Mickey Rooney. The pretty student Tom had called his girlfriend was about to become a big movie star herself. Her name was Ava Gardner.

Later, Tom wrote to Ava in Hollywood, reminding her of those days at Atlantic Christian. She answered and said she remembered him. They exchanged several letters and when Tom went away to college, Ava agreed to be sweetheart of his fraternity.

After college, Tom went to Hollywood himself and worked as a publicist on one of Ava's pictures, *My Forbidden Past*. He moved on to become a publicist for Columbia Pictures in New York before returning to school to get his doctorate in psychology and settling into a practice in Ft. Lauderdale, Florida.

But Tom still kept up with Ava and her career. He began collecting material about her. He compiled scrapbooks for each year of her career, gathered more than 10,000 still photographs from her movie sets, and collected posters and audio cassettes from every movie and video cassettes from most of them.

When Tom visited Ava in London in the late seventies, he told her that he wanted to give his collection to an institution in her honor. She suggested it should be in North Carolina, her home state. Tom was thinking of giving it to a college until he visited Johnston County to see Ava's birthplace.

The big house where Ava was born in the Brogden community 6 miles east of Smithfield was still standing but in disrepair. The teacherage where she lived from ages two to thirteen while her mother taught school was being used as a community social hall. In 1981, Tom bought the teacherage, renovated it, moved his collection into it, and opened the Ava Gardner Museum in 1982.

The museum is open every summer, free of charge. Ava movies are available on video. For more information, call (919) 934-2176.

Ham and Yam Festival

If North Carolina's primary dish is barbecue, the second, surely, is country ham – ham cured in various ways with salt, pepper, sugar, and smoke so that it does not require refrigeration. Some country ham is served baked, but usually it is sliced and fried in huge slabs and served with red-eye gravy, a meat grease with a dollop of coffee that forms a red eye in the center.

Perhaps the best-known country hams in America are produced in Smithfield, Virginia, but Smithfield, North Carolina, too, is a center of country ham production. Five processors are to be found in and around the town. People in Smithfield, North Carolina, have always claimed that their hams are better than the more famous hams made by their Virginia neighbors, and in 1985 they issued a challenge to a taste-off. Virginia accepted and thus was born the Ham and Yam Festival.

Some people maintain that pitting Virginia hams against North Carolina hams is like pitting apples against oranges, because the hams are so different. Virginia hams are long-shanked (with butts attached), cured with salt, smoked for a week, and aged for six months by law. North Carolina hams are a hodgepodge but generally they are short-shanked, cured with salt and sugar, and air-dried without smoke for a minimum of eighty days.

Nevertheless, in that first contest, judged by university food scientists, North Carolina hams took three out of four categories. The second year, Virginia hams fared better but North Carolina hams still took more awards. After that year, Virginia declined to compete again, and other ham producers across North Carolina were invited to join in a statewide contest, thought to be the stiffest in the country.

What do yams have to do with all this? Well, in addition to producing hams, Johnston County grows more sweet potatoes (wrongly called yams) than any other county in the United States, and it could not afford to ignore them in the festival built around the ham contest. Besides, some say that hogs fed on sweet potatoes make the finest hams.

Plenty of country ham biscuits are sold on the streets during the festival, which is held the third weekend in April. A country ham dinner and breakfast are also served. Call (919) 934-0887.

Nash

Bailey

Country Doctor Museum

In rural North Carolina, the country doctor was a greatly revered and highly depended-upon person. Almost always male, he often covered a large territory, did much of his work in his patients' homes, and treated every ailment known or imagined.

Doctors in rural areas are like other doctors now, seeing patients only in their offices or hospitals, but the memory of the old-time doctors lives on at the Country Doctor Museum on Vance Street in Bailey.

The museum was created in 1968, ironically by four female doctors, Josephine Newell, Gloria Graham, Rose Pulley, and Josephine Melchior, all from medical families. All of them had old medical equipment that had been passed down to them, and they thought it ought to be preserved and displayed.

Two former doctors' offices were moved to the site and joined to create the three-room museum. One room is a replica of an old-time doctor's office, another is a pharmacy, and the third contains old equipment ranging from early stethoscopes and microscopes to primitive dental equipment and bleeding instruments. Behind the museum is an herb garden that is a replica of the Medicinal Garden in Padua, Italy. For information about the museum hours, call (919) 235-4165.

Rocky Mount

Where Jim Thorpe Lost His Gold Medals

Jim Thorpe, an Oklahoma Indian who was described as "the greatest athlete in the world," became the first person to win both the decathlon and the pentathlon in the 1912 Olympics. The gold medals were later taken back because Thorpe had played professional baseball. Thorpe, who later gained more fame as a football player, made his professional baseball debut in 1909 with the Rocky Mount Railroaders while a student at Carlisle Institute. The park where he played for two seasons no longer exists, but it was on Franklin Street behind Braswell Memorial Library.

New Hanover

Kure Beach

Oldest Fishing Pier on the East Coast

L.C. Kure built the first fishing pier into the Atlantic Ocean in 1923, using timbers cut nearby. The pier was 16 feet wide and 120 feet long, and it fell in a storm the first year.

The following year, Kure rebuilt his pier with concrete posts rein-forced with railroad iron, doubling the length and width. It has since been damaged by hurricanes eleven times and rebuilt every time.

In 1952, Bill Robertson, then Kure's son-in-law, bought the pier and with relentless promotion made it into a big attraction, the most popular fishing pier on the coast. Three phenomenal months of fishing in the fall of 1957 didn't hurt any. People hauled fish off the pier in wheelbarrows. In a single day, more than 80,000 fish were caught from the pier.

Bill, who died in 1988, wrote a book about the pier called

Man! You Should Have Been Here Last Week. His son Mike now operates the pier.

Seabreeze

World's Oldest Elephant

Although they are generally believed to be long-lived creatures, elephants in the wild live less than fifty years. In captivity, they sometimes live longer. Matteau, a female Asian elephant, was fifty-five when George Tregembo traded four rheas, South American

George Tregembo and Matteau, world's oldest elephant
Photo: Greensboro News-Record

ostrichlike birds, for her in 1966. She turned seventy-six in December, 1988, and the Elephant Interest Group says that makes her the oldest elephant in America and one of the oldest that ever lived. The greatest confirmed age for an elephant is seventy years, but an elephant that died in a California amusement park was believed to be seventy-eight.

Matteau, who weighs nearly five tons, is a familiar sight along-side US-421 south of Wilmington, where during daylight hours in spring, summer, and fall she serves as an attention grabber for George Tregembo's Tote-Em-In Zoo and house of wonders.

George grew up in Maine with dreams of collecting curiosities and exotic animals. He started collecting relics and oddities when he fought in the South Pacific during World War II. When he returned home, he opened a small roadside attraction, but because of bad weather and few tourists, he moved to North Carolina in 1953.

At that time, his zoo had twenty-one species. It now has 130. His collections of oddities fill several buildings and include relics of primitive people from the South Pacific, Africa, South America, and Alaska, war material, Presidential chairs, ancient art objects, and natural wonders such as fossilized dinosaur footprints and the world's largest moth.

A single fee is charged for entrance to the zoo and the collections. Matteau, a gentle creature, can be seen for free. Her handler, James Dinkins, who is the same age as Matteau, sells vegetables for visitors to feed her. Matteau likes almost all fruits and vegetables but refuses peanuts.

"She'll just take 'em and throw 'em down," says George. "She says, 'I'm not working for peanuts.'"

For more information, call (919) 791-0472.

Wilmington

Oldest Little Theater in North America

The Thalian Association, founded in 1788, is the oldest amateur theater group in North America. It is the resident company of Thalian Hall, one of the nation's oldest opera houses. The hall, which faces Princess Street, is a wing of the white-columned City Hall on Third Street.

The theater, with its double balconies and elaborate gilded ornamentation, has seen performances by Lillian Russell, Buffalo

Bill Cody, John Philip Sousa, Oscar Wilde, Marian Anderson, and the Ziegfeld Follies. The ghost of one performer who played there, James O'Neill, famous actor of the last century and father of playwright Eugene O'Neill, is believed to haunt the theater.

"I've never seen him and I don't think anybody has," says the theater's assistant director, Phillip Cumber, "but we've heard him bumping and thumping around."

Strange things are always happening at the theater and are inevitably blamed on James.

Seances have been held to try to rouse James and other ghosts, but none has succeeded. During a rehearsal in 1966, though, cast members saw three figures clad in Victorian clothing watching from the upper balcony. When company members got to the balcony to investigate, the figures were gone, but three seats were turned down as if somebody had been sitting in them.

Tours of the theater are available Tuesday-Saturday, 10:00 A.M.- 3:00 P.M., for a small fee. For information about productions, call (919) 763-3398, or write the Thalian Society, P.O. Box 1111, Wilmington, NC 28402.

The Children's Battleship

The Battleship U.S.S. *North Carolina* was headed for the scrap heap when school children all across the state joined in a campaign to save it in the early sixties. The money they raised helped bring the ship to the state as a memorial to veterans.

Now permanently docked on the Cape Fear River across from downtown Wilmington, the *North Carolina*, which fought in the major Pacific battles of World War II, may be toured for a small fee. From June through Labor Day, a sound and light show telling the ship's history is presented nightly at 9:00 P.M. for an extra fee. Signs direct the way to the ship from US-421 and 17. For more information, call (919) 762-1829.

Girl Buried in Keg of Rum

In 1857, Silas Martin, a ship's captain, set out from Wilmington on an around-the-world voyage. With him went his thirty-four-year-old son John and twenty-four-year-old daughter Nancy, whose pet family name was Nance. At sea, Nancy grew sick and died. Her grieving father had her body folded into a barrel of rum so that it

Children's battleship, U.S.S. North Carolina.

would be preserved until he could bury her at home.

Before Captain Martin could get back, his son was washed overboard during a storm and lost, his body never recovered despite a long search. When Martin finally did make it back to Wilmington, he buried his daughter still in the cask of rum. He was buried beside her four years later.

Nance's grave in Oakdale Cemetery is marked with a stone made to resemble a cross made of logs, next to the larger family marker. The cemetery, which contains many other interesting graves dating back to 1855, is at 520 North Fifteenth Street. The most interesting graves have special markers, and a free itinerary of them can be picked up at the cemetery office at the entrance. For more information, call Oakdale Cemetery at (919) 762-5682.

America's Largest Living Christmas Tree

Every year since 1929, city workers have spent days stringing lights and Spanish moss on a 300-year-old water oak that serves as the community Christmas tree. The 80-foot-tall tree has a limb spread of 110 feet, and nearly 5,000 colored lights are required to decorate it. For more than half a century, Wilmington has proclaimed it America's largest living Christmas tree. The tree, on US-117, two blocks north of Fourth Street, is lighted nightly from the second week in December until New Year's Day.

East's Biggest Film Studio

Filmmaker Dino de Laurentiis discovered Wilmington in 1983 when he came to make *Firestarter* at Orton Plantation, a popular tourist attraction, especially in the spring when Wilmington holds its annual Azalea Festival.

So taken with Wilmington was De Laurentiis that he chose the city as the site for his new movie studio, the largest east of Hollywood. He built it on thirty-two acres on Twenty-third Street near the airport. It included seven sound stages, a commissary, a back lot, and production offices and employed 700 people before DEG Corporation, started by De Laurentiis, fell into financial difficulties and went into reorganization under bankruptcy laws in 1987.

Twenty-eight movies were made at the studio before that, many of them with major stars. Among the films were *Crimes of the Heart, No Mercy, Blue Velvet, Manhunter, Maximum Overdrive, Year of the Dragon,* and the TV miniseries "Noble House" and "Windmills of the Gods."

Five movies were made at the studio in 1988 by major production companies renting the facilities. Early in 1989, the studio remained in the hands of investment bankers, and its future was uncertain.

Onslow

Jacksonville

World's Oldest Putt Putt

The Putt Putt miniature golf course on LeJeune Boulevard was the second built and is the oldest in existence. Putt Putt creator Don Clayton built the course in the fall of 1954. A metal sign he nailed onto a pine tree offering a free pass for a hole-in-one on hole eighteen is still there, now embedded in the tree that grew around it. For more on Putt Putt, see Fayetteville in Cumberland County.

Pamlico

Oriental

Croaker Festival

Croakers are small saltwater fish that make a strange croaking noise when removed from the water. Favored for the taste and texture of their flesh, they are common in North Carolina coastal waters.

Unfortunately, they aren't common at all when Oriental, a quaint town known more for sailing than fishing, holds its Croaker Festival. But the ladies of Oriental's Junior Woman's Club didn't realize that when they started their festival on the July 4th weekend in 1978 and made a croaker fishing contest one of the events.

"We didn't know croakers are not running that time of the year," says Linda Carrow, one of the organizers. "All you can catch are these little tiny ones."

So the fishing contest was dropped and that left almost no role in the festivities for croakers at all. Even the Methodist church fish fry features trout.

But the Junior Woman's Club forges gamely on with its croaker-less salute to croakers nonetheless, staging beauty contests, raft and canoe races, an arts and crafts show, a street dance, and other entertainments. Sailing races are also held in conjunction with the event. For more information, call (919) 249-1555.

Pasquotank

Elizabeth City

Soybean Festival

It's not easy to build a festival around soybeans. After all, they're used primarily for making cooking oil, feeding livestock, and making vegetable meal to be added to other food products. You can't put on a soybean supper and draw much of a crowd.

Some years back, somebody got the idea that roasted soybeans might sell as well as roasted peanuts. They didn't. And you can find out why by sampling some at the Soybean Festival.

Still, it seemed like a good idea for Elizabeth City to honor soybeans, because the first commercial plantings of the Oriental crop in the United States were made near the town in the last century, and the first soybean processing plant in the country was built here in 1912. Soybeans have since become one of the state's and nation's biggest crops and a primary export commodity.

"It's quite a lot to celebrate and commemorate," says Don Baker, a county farm agent who helped organize the event.

The festival is held in January at Elizabeth State University on NC-34. Farm equipment is displayed and country music is performed. For more information, call Don Baker at (919) 338-3954.

Home of World's Greatest Pool Shooter

Luther Lassiter started shooting pool at age thirteen on a friend's homemade backyard table. He perfected his game at the YMCA and at a downtown pool hall called City Billiards. By the time he was in high school, where he picked up the name Wimpy for his hamburger-eating ability, he was practicing for seven or eight hours a day and pool shooters were coming from many counties around to try to beat him.

Wimpy's parents tried to talk him into going to college, but he refused. "Pool had me," he explained years later. "Hell, I wanted to play pool."

And that he did, traveling North Carolina and Virignia to play the best pool shooters for money. Later, he became a professional and was World Straight Pool Champion for eight straight years in the sixties and early seventies. He was also World 9-Ball Champion and All-Around World Champion. In 1983, at age sixty-four, he beat Minnesota Fats, Willie Mosconi, and Jimmy Caras in the Legendary Pocket Billiards Stars Tournament on ESPN.

Wimpy died of a heart attack at age sixty-nine in October 1988. His body was found beside his pool table in a little building behind his family home at 930 Pearl Street, where he had lived his entire life.

Weeksville

America's Only Blimp Works

People in Pasquotank County have once again become accustomed to seeing huge presences passing overhead.

During World War II, the U.S. Navy built two monstrous hangars beside the Pasquotank River on NC-34 between Weeksville and Elizabeth City, and there they built blimps for the Navy to use as observation decks and submarine chasers. The Navy phased out blimps in 1962, and for many years the hangars stood idle. But in 1983, Airships Industries took over one of the monstrous structures and began producing blimps once again, mostly to be used as advertising vehicles. The company also set up a school to train crews to fly the big, helium-filled airships.

In 1988, the Navy revived its interest in blimps, this time to serve as sophisticated radar stations that will remain in the air for weeks at a time. Airships Industries won the contract to build the first experimental airship, which is to be 423 feet long and 150 feet high, designed to fly as high as 10,000 feet at a top speed of 90 miles per hour. The crew area will have three decks.

In 1989, company officials were talking not only of building many more military blimps, but of building monstrous travel palaces to carry passengers on luxurious flights, as dirigibles did earlier in this century.

Pender

Hampstead

Mac Millis's Outer Space Venus's-Flytrap Nursery

Venus's-flytrap, the most dramatic of all the earth's insect-eating plants, grows naturally in only one place, an area within about a 75-mile radius of Hampstead. McKinley Millis, usually called Mac, remembers playing with them as a child growing up on Harrison Creek, sticking sticks into them, trying to make their spinelike teeth shut, the way the plant traps insects it devours.

"We called 'em eye catchers," Mac remembers. "Looked like a person's eye."

Mac was born in 1911, and in the days of his boyhood livestock was allowed to range freely and crops were fenced. Woods were burned regularly to clear undergrowth and create forage for the stock. Burning the woods created a prime environment for the Venus's-flytrap, which grew prolifically in the cleared, damp areas.

The plant, now protected by law, is endangered due to poaching, development, modern tree farming techniques, and other factors,

and seeing one in the wild is a rare treat. But plenty are to be
seen at Mac Millis's small nursery on US-17 at the intersection of
NC-210 (the nursery is named for Mac's daughter, Marie).

Mac began experimenting with growing flytraps from seeds
nearly thirty years ago and became one of the first commercial
growers of the plant. How he grows them, he won't tell.

"I got a lot of secrets I don't give out," he says.

Mac, incidentally, believes that the plant got its name because
the seed actually came from Venus.

Southeastern North Carolina is dotted with mysterious, shallow,
round craters, most of them water-filled, called the Carolina Bays.
Some scientists believe the craters were caused by a meteor shower
long ago, and Mac believes that.

"My great-great-granddaddy remembered when they fell," he
says.

He also believes that the seeds of the flytrap, a plant with a space-
monsterish look about it, arrived on those meteors by way of Venus.

If there are flytraps on Venus, there must be flies there, too,
right?

"I guess so," says Mac. "No telling what's there. Nobody never
been there to find out, have they?"

Spot Festival

The spots celebrated in Hampstead every year aren't the kind
you see in front of your eyes when you're dizzy, or the kind you get
on your clothes when you drip ketchup or gravy. These are the spots
that swim in the ocean, the ones you can eat, and eating is the
major event of the Spot Festival.

The spot is the most bountiful fish in North Carolina's coastal
waters. Spots are small, silver-colored, with a distinctive black spot
near the gills. They are a favorite of sports fishermen, who sometimes catch them by the bucketfull, especially in spring and fall.

Spots weren't caught commercially until the thirties, but by the
fifties they had become the biggest-selling fish in the South.

Three seafood packing plants grew in Hampstead, processing
tons of spots every year. In 1964, to draw attention to the
community's claim to being "the seafood capital of the Carolinas"
and to celebrate the beginning of the fall run of spots, the Spot
Festival was begun to raise money for community projects.

Held on the third weekend in September, the festival is a three-
day event with beauty pageants, a golf tournament, pig picking,

an arts and crafts show, an auction, and entertainment by popular groups. But the big event is the fish fry at the community building, which begins at 11:00 A.M. on Saturday and continues until 6:00 P.M. More than 3,500 pounds of spots are cooked. For more information, call (919) 270-4470.

Scott's Hill

Haunted Plantation

From 1795 to 1975, Poplar Grove Plantation was in the Foy family. In the early 1800s, Poplar Grove became one of North Carolina's first and biggest peanut-producing plantations. The original house burned and was rebuilt in 1850 by Joseph M. Foy, a wealthy and influential man in the state. His son, Joseph T. Foy, took over the plantation at age fifteen upon his father's death.

In 1975, the plantation was bought by a nonprofit foundation, which restored it as a national historic site and opened it to tours. But one member of the Foy family refuses to move.

She is Aunt Nora, wife of the young Joseph Foy. She moved into the house as a young woman following the Civil War and lived there until her death in 1923. Nora was a lively young woman who etched her name and her husband's into a window pane of the house on their wedding day. In later years, Nora became a pipe-smoking,

Poplar Grove, a haunted plantation

joke-cracking character who was community postmistress. Since her death, her presence has continued to pervade Poplar Grove. She can sometimes be heard pacing in her upstairs room. Staff members tell of tricks that Aunt Nora, as she is known, sometimes plays on them. And occasionally, when all lights are out in the house, a mysterious glow can be seen in the window of Nora's room, particularly near Christmas.

Each year at Halloween, the Plantation conducts haunted house tours and other events in honor of Aunt Nora, including dinner featuring such dishes as sliced tongue and beef hearts with blood gravy and slime pie. The Plantation is on US-17, north of Wilmington. For more information, call (919) 686-9886.

Perquimans

Hertford

Oldest House in North Carolina

A brick house on a rise within sight of the Perquimans River, built about 1685 by Joseph Scott, an early Quaker who became a magistrate and legislator, is the oldest house in North Carolina.

The Governors Council met at the house in the 1690s, and the Colonial Assembly was convened in it in 1697.

Since then, the house has had more than thirty owners. In 1973, it was sold to the Perquimans County Restoration Association, which restored it and opened it as a historic site in 1981. Called the Newbold-White House, after late owners, it is on State Road 1336, 1.5 miles off US-17 bypass, southeast of Hertford. Open Monday-Saturday, 10:00 A.M.-4:30 P.M., March 1 through Thanksgiving. It may be seen only by appointment the rest of the year. For more information, call (919) 426-7567.

Largest U.S. Cherrybark Oak

One of the largest trees in North Carolina, the cherrybark oak on Lucky Cartwright's property on State Road 1329, two miles south of the Woodville community, is the national champion of its species. The tree is 120 feet tall with a crown spread of 126 feet. Its trunk is 29 feet in circumference.

Pitt

Ayden

The Collard Festival

Ayden is probably the only town in the United States with collards growing on Main Street. Collards are tall, tough greens that thrive in the colder months in the South and thus are prized as a fresh vegetable when few are to be had. At one time almost every rural home in the South had a collard patch out back.

Collards have to be cooked a long time to make them tender enough to eat, and it has been said that a single pot of them cooking is enough to smell up a whole county.

Despite the fact that collards grow on Main Street and Bum's Restaurant has collards on the menu every day, folks in Ayden aren't known to grow or eat more collards than anybody else. So why do they celebrate collards every year on the second weekend in September?

Blame it on a Yankee.

Lois Theuring moved to Ayden when her husband's company transferred him to nearby Greenville. She frequently wrote articles for the local weekly newspaper, the *News-Leader*. She also hated collards. In one article that she wrote about the things she liked about the South, she closed every paragraph with a disparaging remark about collards.

As it happened, some people in town were then thinking about organizing a festival to compete with nearby Grifton's highly successful Shad Festival, and a local businessman, Willis Manning, wrote a letter to the editor asking for ideas. He closed it by facetiously suggesting that Mrs. Theuring might agree to organize a collard festival.

Lois Theuring surprised everybody by doing just that. She organized the first one in 1975 and it was a great success. She moved back to Ohio the following year, and the last anybody in Ayden heard she still hated collards.

The festival she organized grows bigger every year. It includes a parade, carnival, and numerous other events. The most popular event is the collard-eating contest. It usually isn't a pretty sight, since not all the contestants are able to hold their collards.

The all-time collard-eating champion is Desmond Rogers, a 340-pound pickup truck dealer from Snow Hill, who has won the contest every time he has entered. He once downed six and a quarter pounds of collards in a single sitting.

Greenville

World's Largest Flue-cured Tobacco Show and Festival

Flue-cured tobacco is tobacco that is picked one leaf at a time and barn-cured with heat, as opposed to burly tobacco, which is cut by the stalk and hung to air dry.

Pitt County produces more flue-cured tobacco than any other place on earth. It brings $60 million a year to the local economy. So it should be no surprise that the biggest show of tobacco farming equipment is held in Greenville, the Pitt County seat. And since so many farmers and their families came to the show and were looking for entertainment, the Tobacco Festival evolved from the show.

The festival, held each year in the week before Thanksgiving, features many events at many locations, including clogging, country music, pig pickings, quilt and antique shows, pipe smoking, tobacco spitting, and tobacco grading contests.

But the biggest event is the naming of the Tobacco Farmer of the Year for the five-state flue-cured tobacco growing belt, and the picking of the year's most perfect bundle of tobacco, which is always on display.

For more information, call (919) 752-4101.

Grifton

The Shad Festival

Shad are saltwater fish, members of the herring family, that, like salmon, return to spawn in the fresh water streams where they hatched. In late winter and early spring, they move by the thousands up the Neuse River and into creeks such as Pitchkettle, Grindle, and Contentnea.

Two types of shad make this migration: the hickory, which averages one to two pounds, and the white (or American), which averages three pounds but grows much larger. Hickory shad are predominant.

Both varieties are prized primarily for their roe, which is

traditionally fried with onions or scrambled with eggs in eastern North Carolina.

Only small samples of shad can be found at the Shad Festival. The big fish fry features herring filets. The big fish stew contains rockfish. Shad, alas, are entirely too bony for most folks' taste. Festival organizers say a shad can be made edible by baking it at least six hours, thus softening the bones. Others say it takes half a day and isn't worth the effort.

Shad may or may not be good to eat, but it is a good enough excuse for Grifton, a town of 2,400 people, to hold a five-day fling the third weekend in April (unless that is Easter), as it has been doing since 1970.

The activities include a parade; a fishing contest; a fish-lying contest; canoe races; foot races; beauty pagaents; a street dance; clogging; an arts and crafts competition; tennis, archery, and golf tournaments; a barbecue and Shad-O games, based on Bingo. For information, call Janet Haseley at (919) 524-4356 or The Shad Festival at (919) 524-4075.

Robeson

Maxton

Chief Wise Owl's Drowning Creek Reservation and America's Biggest Belly

Chief Wise Owl, who eschews his given name, "the white man's name," won a contest sponsored by the *National Enquirer* in 1986 to find America's biggest belly. His measured 111 inches.

This was not the first contest in which Wise Owl, who has weighed as much as 859 pounds, emerged victorious. He has won many eating and drinking contests. He once ate forty-five hot dogs at one sitting. "Most beer I ever drank at one time was nine quarts," he says with pride.

Because of his size, Wise Owl, a Tuscarora Indian, rarely leaves his small house on a country road off NC-71 north of Maxton near the Lumber River. A big sign identifies the house and the land on which it sits as the Drowning Creek Reservation.

Wise Owl has subdivided three acres of the land into 21,600,000 square-inch plots, which he sells through advertisements in national publications at $20 each. Buyers get a picture of the chief and a certificate making them honorary members of his tribe along with their deeds.

From his house, Wise Owl, who also proclaims himself a medicine man, sells "Indian" blankets at $39 each (these, too, he advertises in national publications). The factory-made blankets, 50 percent polyester and 50 percent acrylic, come with personal blessings from Wise Owl.

Jetliner Graveyard

They loom unexpectedly in the piney flatlands, jetliners, some in Easter egg colors, far from any hubs of commercial aviation.

What are they doing in this isolated, rural setting?

Closer examination shows that most are not whole, for here at the spacious Laurinburg-Maxton Airport, a former military base for training glider pilots, a Charlotte aircraft company operates a jetliner junkyard. Worn-out jetliners are brought here and stripped of parts, while others are brought to be restored and sold.

The jetliners attract a lot of attention, especially from passing private pilots, who frequently stop just to see what they are doing there.

Mechanics who strip the planes complain of only one problem from working in the country. The planes become havens for the diamondback and timber rattlesnakes that are so common in the area.

The airport is on Air Base Road, about five miles off US-74 between Maxton and Laurinburg. Follow highway signs.

Pembroke

Lost Colony Found?

The first attempt at a permanent English settlement in America ended in mystery. The settlers on Roanoke Island, near Manteo, disappeared, leaving only the word "Croatan" carved on a tree, and became known as the Lost Colony.

Many Lumbee Indians believe the Lost Colony was never lost, that it simply joined with their ancestors and moved inland, the two groups eventually melding into one.

As evidence, they point to reports of early settlers along the Lumber River encountering native people with blue eyes and fair

skin who spoke English words. As further proof, they point
to the common Lumbee family names, Chavis, Dare, Lowry,
Locklear, and Oxendine – all also names of settlers in the Lost
Colony.

Lumbees number more than 40,000 in Robeson County, perhaps
50,000 nationwide, and are the only Indians to hold onto their
native lands without being forced onto a reservation. They make
up perhaps a tenth of all American Indians, but have never been
recognized as a tribe by the federal government.

In the seventies a resurgence of Indian pride swept through the
Lumbees, and it is manifested in the Lumbee Homecoming held
on the July 4th weekend each year. Lumbee beauty queens are
chosen; a parade is held; and there are demonstrations of crafts and
Indian dances.

From late June until August an outdoor drama, *Strike at the
Wind*, about Lumbee hero Henry Berry Lowery, is presented
Thursday-Saturday at the Lakeside Amphitheater at Riverside
Country Club a half mile off US-74 west of Pembroke. For more
information, call (919) 521-3112.

Proctorville

America's Smallest Public Library

Proctorville, an isolated rural community off NC-130, once
thrived. "We used to have a lot of stores here but they burned
down," says Beatrice Warwick, the town librarian.

Now there's only Babe Loflin's Store, the volunteer fire department, the small post office, and the library, a tiny brick structure
built by W.R. (Mr. Will) Sulls during the Depression.

A branch of the Robeson County Public Library, the Proctorville
Library has long claimed the title of America's smallest public
library. It is open only on Thursdays from 3:30 to 5:00 P.M., and
few adults use it. "Everybody works and they can't get off the time
I've got it open," says Beatrice.

Not even many schoolchildren come for books during the school
year. "It's better in the summertime," says Beatrice. "Summertime
the children really come and get 'em."

How many volumes does the library boast? "A pile of 'em,"
says Beatrice. "Oh, I reckon there's over 300. Why, there might be
500 out there."

Raemon

Yvonne Leow's Love Garden

Yvonne Leow has heard voices since childhood. The voices told her to write poems, prayers, and songs, and in 1977 she became the first person from her country, Guyana, on the north-central coast of South America, to record a gospel album. That year voices also told her to buy an acre and a half of land on the side of US-501 south of Laurinburg and build a garden of love to Christ.

She built her garden of concrete blocks, ceramic figures, wrought iron arches, and thousands of brightly colored plastic flowers. She also constructed an altar, painted red, green, and yellow, to which she regularly invites gospel singing groups to perform for free.

In her nearby trailer, artificial flowers adorn every surface. "When I sleep, I sleep in a garden," says Yvonne. "It is a garden of love. All these flowers, to me, they're just like people. We are the flowers of the earth. We are in a garden of love."

Visitors are welcome. In the trailer, Yvonne sells her poems, albums, prayers, anointing oils, cleansing and purifying herbal baths, and teas bearing her picture and perfume called "Road to Happiness."

Red Springs

Flora MacDonald Highland Games

As a young woman in Scotland, Flora MacDonald became a heroine. The Scots, led by Prince Charles, pretender to the throne, were fighting the English. They suffered a crushing defeat at Culloden Moor in April 1746, and Prince Charles retreated to the island of Benbecula, where he was quickly surrounded and trapped. Flora came to the rescue by disguising the prince in petticoat, dress, and bonnet and leading him to safety.

In 1774, Flora joined the emigration to this country and settled in southeastern North Carolina, where she was welcomed by earlier Scottish settlers. She soon became involved in the American Revolution, but as a Tory she opposed it.

Nevertheless, she has remained a heroine to Americans of Scottish descent, a great many of whom reside in southeastern North Carolina. A college (now defunct) was named for her, and to continue her memory, a nonprofit group was formed in 1977 to sponsor the Flora MacDonald Highland Games and Gathering of Clans.

Each year on the first weekend in October, several thousand people gather to wear kilts and tartans, listen to the pipes and drums, watch Scottish dances and traditional Highland athletic contests such as the caber toss – pitching a 20-foot, 100-pound pole – and the sheaf toss – throwing a sack of straw with a pitchfork.

The event is held in a field on State Road 1001, 3 miles north of Red Springs, off NC-71. For more information, call G.T. Ammons at (919) 843-4139.

Sampson

Clinton

The Ugly Pickup Truck Contest

A merchants group was looking for something to draw people to downtown Clinton when Gene Pierce, a furniture store owner, suggested holding an ugly pickup truck contest.

"As many ugly trucks as we've got around here, that's got to be something that would work for us," he said.

Work it did. That first contest not only drew two dozen entries; it also attracted newspaper reporters and television crews, and the merchants decided to make it an annual event held the first Saturday in November.

The contest attracts trucks from as far away as Virginia, South Carolina, and Georgia, and they are ugly indeed. "Some of 'em are just terrible," says Pierce. "If you threw something in the back of some of 'em, it would just go right to the ground. I'd be scared to ride in most of 'em."

The only rules are that the trucks must have valid inspection stickers and be driven into and out of the Lisbon Street parking lot where the contest is held. Call (919) 592-1961.

Spivey's Corner

National Hollerin' Contest

Ermon Godwin's granddaddy loved to holler.

"Most every man out in the country in those days did holler," Ermon says. "But some of them were better known for hollerin', and my grandfather, Bud Godwin, was a well known hollerin' man."

One day in 1969, Ermon, a banker in Dunn, asked John Thomas, a friend who worked at the local radio station, if he'd ever heard of the area's tradition of hollerin' as a means of communication in the days before telephones and easy transportation.

John thought he was kidding, so Ermon found a hollerin' man, George Demming, and got him to holler for him. John put George on the radio and after he hollered, remarked "We ought to have a hollerin' contest."

That was the beginning of the National Hollerin' Contest, one of the most popular of America's offbeat events, drawing more than 10,000 people annually to Spivey's Corner, a crossroads community on US-421, 11 miles south of Dunn.

The contest has attracted international attention, and many of the winners have appeared on Johnny Carson's "Tonight Show."

Lots of screamers and yellers show up each year, but enough of the old timers to whom hollerin' was an art come to make it interesting.

But Dewey Jackson, an old timer who won the first contest in 1969, wonders how long the old hollerin' tradition can last at the contest.

"It's a lot of these here young'uns a-tryin' to holler," he says with contempt. "They ain't much hollerin' to it."

The hollerin' contest, held the first Saturday in June at Midway High School, includes a whistling contest, fox-horn-blowing contest, conch-blowing contest, clogging, music, and a barbecue. For more information, call Ermon Godwin at (919) 892-4133.

Turkey

Claude Moore's Cabin Museum

Claude Moore is a former school principal, retired history professor, newspaper columnist, and lecturer who enjoys few things more than dressing up in his Confederate general's uniform and leading people through his Cabin Museum.

Claude believes in making history tangible and throughout his life he collected pieces of it. In the late fifties, he bought a log cabin built in Duplin County in 1770 and moved it to Sampson County to house his collection. In 1977, he moved it again to its present location 3 miles north of Turkey (turn at Turkey's blinking light off NC-24) on his great-grandfather's home place, where he now lives.

He also moved part of an 1859 plantation house to the site, restored it, and opened both buildings as a museum. Thousands of items pertaining to the history of eastern North Carolina are on display, including turpentining equipment, barrel-making tools, and many Confederate items. Claude is especially proud of an original Matthew Brady photograph of Robert E. Lee.

The museum may be seen free by appointment. Call Claude at (919) 533-3142.

Turkey Day

People from Turkey get used to the inevitable jokes, but most of them are proud of their town, which got its name from the abundance of wild turkeys in the area when the town sprang up in the last century. In 1987, they expressed that pride by holding Turkey Day, an annual event on the Saturday before Thanksgiving. Events include a parade, a gospel singing, and a barbecue that features pork, not turkey.

Scotland

Laurinburg

Spaghetti's Grave

Forenzio Concippio, a carnival worker, got himself clobbered with a tent stake and killed in 1911. His father made a down payment on a funeral and told the undertaker he'd return with the remainder of the money and burial instructions. He didn't and for the next sixty-two years Forenzio's mummified body hung first on an embalming room wall, then in the garage at McDougald's Funeral Home in Laurinburg. The body, which became known as Spaghetti because local people couldn't pronounce Concippio's name properly, became quite a tourist attraction, drawing people from all over the country.

In 1973, it drew the attention of a New York congressman of Italian ancestry who raised a storm of protest, and the funeral home finally buried Spaghetti in Hillside Cemetery on Hillside Street, just off US-401. The grave is on the right, beside the street, just past the cemetery entrance and bears a marker placed by the funeral home.

Dizzy Gillespie Jazz Hall of Fame

For the time being, it amounts to little more than a cap, a cape, and a few other personal items in the gymnasium of Laurinburg Institute, but Frank McDuffie, Jr. has great hopes.

McDuffie now heads the black prep school started by his grand-father in 1904, the school from which famed jazz musician Dizzy Gillespie, a Cheraw, SC native, graduated in 1935. He wants to establish the John Birks (that's Dizzy's real name) Gillespie Center for Cultural Change and Jazz Hall of Fame on his campus.

The center would be a place for jazz research and seminars and would include a museum of jazz recordings and memorabilia and a Hall of Fame honoring great jazz musicians.

If you should stop by to see Dizzy's cap and cape, also check the school's Sports Hall of Fame in the gym. The tiny school's alumni include Charlie Smith, the first black basketball player for the University of North Carolina; Sam Jones of the Boston Celtics; Jimmy Walker of the Detroit Pistons; Wes Covington, a major league baseball player; and Willie McCray of the San Francisco 49ers. The school is on McGirt Bridge Road, just off US-15-501. For more information, call (919) 276-0684.

Indian Museum of Carolinas

Dr. David McLean was a missionary in Africa for twenty-five years before he returned to this country to teach anthropology at St. Andrews Presbyterian College in Laurinburg.

Once back in North Carolina, he took an avid interest in the Indians who formerly had lived in the area. He began collecting Indian artifacts and came to be able to tell from any artifact which tribe had made it and in which period. He bought some artifacts, traded African artifacts for others, and some were given to him.

As his collection grew over a period of twenty years, he began thinking of building a museum to house it. He opened it in 1968. The museum includes not only artifacts but dioramas showing how Indians of the Southeast lived.

Dr. McLean died in 1980, but his museum at 607 Turnpike Road is open Wednesday and Thursday, 10:00 A.M.-12:00 P.M. and 1:00-4:00 P.M., Sunday, 1:00-4:00 P.M., and other times by appointment. Call (919) 276-4240.

Washington

Creswell

Mike Davenport's Orange Tree

Oranges won't grow in North Carolina and Mike Davenport was well aware of this when in 1965 he brought home from Florida a souvenir orange tree that was little more than a sprig.

Mike, a former blacksmith who before his retirement ran a combination machine shop, gas station, garage, grocery, and funeral home ("We feed the living, bury the dead, make your auto go ahead," was his motto), set the tree out in his backyard nonetheless. When it thrived through a summer, Mike decided to try to keep it alive through winter by enclosing it in plastic and keeping it warm.

That proved to be the beginning of a never-ending struggle. Each year, Mike had to enlarge the enclosure and install new heating sources. Now the orange tree fills its own greenhouse more than 25 feet tall. It is warmed in winter by gas and electric heaters, and elaborate alarms sound if any heating source fails.

Some years, Mike, who turned ninety in 1988, gets as many as a thousand oranges from his tree, but he admits that the average cost per orange is much higher than he would pay in a supermarket. He shares the oranges with friends and neighbors and he is happy to show his tree and antique machinery to visitors. He lives across from the post office in the only brick house on Main Street.

Somerset Homecoming

Inspired by Alex Haley's *Roots*, Dorothy Redford, a social worker from Portsmouth, Virginia, began tracing her family history. Her research led to a reunion in 1986 of descendants of slaves and slave owners at Somerset Place, a state historic site that once was the second largest plantation in North Carolina.

Beginning in 1786, Josiah Collins, an English merchant, used eighty slaves to carve Somerset Place out of swampland on the banks of Lake Phelps. The plantation, maintained by slaves, prospered through three generations of the Collins family until it was plundered and abandoned during the Civil War. The Somerset Place slaves scattered over the East Coast, and their descendants ended up all over the country. The Collins family sold the plantation shortly after the war, and their descendants eventually settled on the West Coast.

After learning that her own forebears had been slaves at Somerset Place, Dorothy Redford began tracking descendants of other slaves there and organized the historic reunion on the anniversary of the arrival of the plantation's first slaves. More than 2,000 people attended the reunion at the restored plantation mansion built by Josiah Collins III in 1829. Among the guests was Alex Haley. The story of Dorothy Redford's search and the reunion is told in her book, Somerset Homecoming, published in 1988.

Somerset Place is on State Road 1168, 6 miles southeast of Creswell. A state historic site, it is open Monday-Saturday, 9:00 A.M.-5:00 P.M., Sunday, 1:00-5:00 P.M., April-October; Tuesday-Saturday, 10:00 A.M.-4:00 P.M., Sunday, 1:00-4:00 P.M., November-March. No admission is charged. Call (919) 797-4560.

Wayne

Mt. Olive

Pickle Town, U.S.A.

All you have to do to find Mt. Olive, people from the town will tell you, is follow your nose. The whole town smells like pickles. It even calls itself Pickle Town, U.S.A.

Pickles are America's favorite preserved fruit or vegetable (there's debate about just which category cucumbers fall into). We each eat nearly nine pounds a year on the average. But nobody loves pickles more than the people of Mt. Olive do. Pickles are the town's major industry.

In 1926, farmers around Mt. Olive found themselves with a cucumber crop they couldn't sell. Some enterprising businessmen in Mt. Olive built a large brine vat and stored the cucumbers in it until they could be sold to an out-of-state pickle packer. Within a few years, the businessmen were making their own pickles.

The Mt. Olive Pickle Co. is now one of the nation's largest, and because of it and the smaller Cates Pickle Co. in nearby Faison, North Carolina and Michigan vie for the honor of being America's largest cucumber-growing state.

Eastern North Carolina farmers plant more than 30,000 acres in cucumbers, and each year the Mt. Olive Pickle Co. buys nearly 750,000 bushels and transforms them into some 25 million jars of pickles. At peak harvesting time in late June and July, cucumbers often come into the plant at the rate of 40,000 bushels a day.

The company makes nearly a third of the fresh cucumbers into pickles immediately. The rest are stored in a thousand huge redwood and cypress brine vats for year-round production.

Visitors may tour the plant Monday through Friday but are discouraged from doing so in peak harvesting time. They receive free pickle badges, balloons, bookmarks, and other pickle paraphernalia, and lucky ones get to meet John Walker, the downhome, Harvard-educated company president who drives a car with a license plate that reads DILLY-O, passes out pickle hats and T-shirts, and rattles off pickle jokes and puns with relish.

Drop-in visitors are welcome, but the company prefers that appointments be made by calling (919) 658-2535. The plant, John Walker likes to say, is at Cucumber and Vine. Make that Witherington and Center.

After the cucumbers are all brined for the year, Mt. Olive celebrates with its annual Pickle Festival, held in late September. People in Mt. Olive say they would be pickled tink to see visitors at their affair. Call (919) 658-3113.

Nahunta

America's Largest Retail Pork Store

Nahunta isn't on highway maps and it's not easy to find, but thousands of North Carolinians regularly make their way there, and many travelers from other states also search it out, all for the same reason: the Nahunta Pork Center.

As a young man, Mack Pierce opened a small slaughterhouse across from his country home to process hogs for barbecue houses and sausage makers. After a dozen years, he decided to open a tiny meat market next to his house. People warned that it would never succeed because it was too far out in the country for customers to find it. But through tireless work and promotion, the reputation of his country hams, sausages, and hickory-smoked bacon began to spread and the store thrived.

The store, which employs forty people and processes an average of a hundred hogs each day, offers only pork, and Mack boasts that nobody sells it fresher.

"Everything you see in the case was walking ten hours ago," he says.

In addition to every imaginable cut of fresh pork, the store also sells brains, chitlins, cracklins, souse, liver pudding, and an item that Eastern North Carolinians call Tom Thumb, a pig's stomach stuffed with sausage and dry-cured.

On Saturdays, Mack offers his customers free country ham and sausage biscuits and beverages, and every year on the store's anniversary he puts on a big show for regular customers, often with big-name country entertainers.

Signs on US-70 west of Goldsboro point the way to Nahunta, also known as Sausage City.

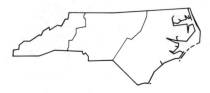

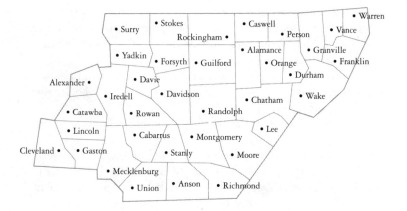

The Piedmont

Alamance

Burlington

Outlet Capital of the South

North Carolina is a state filled with "outlets," stores that purport to offer much lower prices because they are operated by the factories that make the products they sell.

In the beginning, outlets were indeed places where factories sold to the public, often from a corner of the factory, and many such places do exist around the state. Their popularity was so great that stores calling themselves outlets began opening, although they weren't owned by the factories.

In some places, outlet centers sprang up. Burlington, which boasts nearly a hundred (most in two large complexes alongside I-85), has even registered itself as the "Outlet Capital of the South." Tour buses bring shoppers to Burlington from throughout the country.

Other nearby towns also have outlets. Guides to all the outlets can be purchased at newsstands.

Wildlife Museum

The late Dr. Brodie McDade, a Burlington pediatrician, was a big-game hunter who traveled the world stalking his prey. He always returned with trophies.

When his collection of stuffed animals and mounted heads became too large for his home, he filled his clinic with them and delighted in showing them to children, who frequently came in large groups to see them.

The collection eventually grew too big even for Dr. McDade's two-story clinic, and in 1956 he donated it to the town of Burlington for a museum. Money was raised to build a wing onto the new administrative offices of the town's recreation department in City Park to house the collection. It became McDade Wildlife Museum.

The collection includes more than 500 different animals, large and small, all shot by Dr. McDade, who died in 1974. It is one of the largest such collections in the nation. Made up mostly of mounted heads, it also features horns, antlers, the tusks of a huge bull elephant, and many whole animals, including a crocodile, black bear, two leopards, a whitetail deer, and even bald and golden eagles.

The museum at 1333 Overbrook Road is open Monday-Friday, 8:00 A.M.-5:00 P.M., at no charge. For more information, call Burlington City Parks at (919) 222-5030.

Snow Camp

Robert Lindley's Studebaker Rest Home

Back in the days when a great many Southern men identified themselves with the kind of car they drove, Robert Lindley was a Studebaker man.

He just liked Studebakers and always drove one. After the Studebaker Company went out of business in 1966, he didn't see any need to quit driving the cars he loved. So just to be sure he'd always be able to drive one, he started collecting old Studebakers wherever he could find them, in whatever condition they happened to be.

He accumulated about seventy-five around his house in various states of repair, not to mention a few Henry Js and Willys Jeeps. They enable Robert, a lifelong mechanic, to while away his days working on his beloved Studebakers in an old barn stocked full of Studebaker parts.

His Studebaker rest home is on Bethel Church Road. For more information, call (919) 376-3733.

Alexander

Hiddenite

World's Rarest Gemstones

New York mineralogist W.E. Hidden was looking for a source of platinum for inventor Thomas Edison when he came to Alexander County and discovered a pale green variety of the gem spodumene, which came to bear his name. Hiddenite is the world's rarest gem, found on only a few acres in Alexander County.

Those same acres have also borne some of the world's finest emeralds. Farmers who found emeralds while plowing in the 1800s called them green bolts and had little use for them.

Not until the 1960s when property owners began letting treasure hunters dig on their land did the gems of Hiddenite begin attracting national attention.

In 1969, a Lincolnton man, Michael Finger, found a 1,438-carat emerald, the largest ever found in North America.

In 1970, another digger found a large stone 8 feet down and sold it to mine owner Lois Rist for $700. She later sold it to Tiffany and Co. in New York for $7,000. Cut and polished, the stone, called the Carolina Emerald, is now valued at $300,000.

Some of the most productive lands at Hiddenite have been bought by a large mining company and closed to the public. But Carolina Emerald Mines still has nearly four acres open for digging. The mine has a campground and showers and charges a daily fee for digging from sunup to sundown. It's on a gravel road off NC-90 near Hiddenite School.

Cabarrus

Concord

The Buffalo Ranch

Originated by A.B. Cook, The Buffalo Ranch is now owned by Ken and Doug Godley. The ranch has more than just buffaloes; there are exotic breeds of cattle and goats, plus yaks, llamas, zebras, camels, lions, tigers, monkeys, and other animals. Stagecoaches make the 2 1/2-mile trip around the ranch for a small fee.

The ranch, at 3241 NC-49, 1 mile east of US-601, is open April 1 through November 1, Monday-Saturday, 10:00 A.M.-5:30 P.M.; Sunday 1:00-6:00 P.M. The rest of the year, it's open weekends only, weather permitting. The Western Store is open year-round. For information, call (704) 782-2009.

The Nation's First Gold Mine

Conrad Reed was twelve when he found an unusual rock in Little Meadow Creek on his daddy's farm in 1799. It was beautiful, everybody agreed, and the family used it as a doorstop until John Reed took it to a jeweler in 1802. The jeweler realized the seventeen-pound rock was gold but didn't tell Reed. He bought it for $3.50. It was worth $3,500 at the time.

Reed later discovered he'd been cheated by the jeweler, demanded, and got more money. Meanwhile word of the big nugget had spread. It created the country's first gold rush.

John Reed panned for gold only in the creek on his farm in the beginning, but in 1825 it was discovered that the gold was coming from the white quartz so common in the area, and Reed and some associates began digging into the creek banks. In 1831, they started digging North America's first gold mine on the farm. So much gold was taken from mines in the area that the government opened a mint in Charlotte in 1837.

Reed died in 1845, before the California gold rush drew attention away from the North Carolina mines. His mine changed hands many times before it was finally closed in 1912.

In 1971, the 822-acre Reed farm was donated to the state and the old mine was restored and opened as a historic site in 1977. It attracts more than 100,000 visitors annually. A museum offers displays of gold mining equipment and photos and maps of old mines.

A quarter mile of the hand-dug mine that goes 48 feet underground is open for visitors to examine, and the stamp mill used to crush ore from the mine has been restored.

Visitors may pan for gold from April through October, but the ore comes from Cotton Patch Mine, a commercial tourist mine in Stanly County.

The mine is on Reed Mine Road, 2 miles from NC-200, 4 miles off US-601, about 14 miles south of Concord. It is open year round, Monday-Saturday, 9:00 A.M.-5:00 P.M., Sunday, 1:00-5:00 P.M. There is no charge.

Harrisburg

World's Longest Stock-car Race

Stock-car racing is the only major sport to come out of the South. From its beginnings in the forties with moonshine liquor runners in souped-up cars racing each other on bets, the sport grew into a multi-million-dollar business featuring sophisticated racing cars running at high speeds on tracks called "superspeedways" that attracts millions of spectators annually.

Stock-car racers were already running 500-mile races at Darlington when former moonshine runner Curtis Turner, one of the top stock-car racers, teamed with Charlotte businessman Bruton Smith in the late fifties and announced plans to build a mile-and-a-half track in Cabarrus County where they would hold a 600-mile race. Some in the sport believed that both cars and drivers were pushing their limits of endurance at 500-mile races, but the race went on anyway on an unfinished track in 1960.

It was called the World 600. It has remained the only 600-mile race, attracting more than 100,000 people to Charlotte Motor Speedway on US-29, near Harrisburg, north of Charlotte, each Memorial Day weekend. For more information, call (704) 455-2121.

Caswell

Hightowers

Henry Warren's Shangri-la

Henry Warren was a wiry, industrious man who liked to add special touches to the things he did. He built his own house and when he added the sidewalk he embedded in it, in many designs, more than 11,000 arrowheads he'd collected.

In 1969, when he was seventy-seven, Henry started another project. It came about because of another little special touch he'd added, a stone goldfish pond.

"I always wanted a water wheel for that pond," he told an interviewer. "Well, I got it. Then once I had it, I thought I'd build a mill house for it. You know, put it beside the pond and attach the wheel to it.

"I got all that and then I made a miller to turn the wheel. I hooked an electric motor up to the wheel, and it looks like the miller turning the wheel. Well, once I had that, I thought maybe the miller needed a home for his family. So I built that."

The miller's family, of course, needed a store and a church and a school and. . . .

It just kept growing, all in miniature, a whole village built of the white quartz Henry quarried on his farm. It was Henry's own little fantasy land, and appropriately he named it Shangri-la and opened it for all to enjoy. People came by the hundreds to wander through it and snap photographs.

"The kids are the ones who get the most involved in it," Henry said. "I just want them to enjoy it."

Henry kept expanding his village until his death at eighty-five in 1977. Before he died, he requested of his family that his Shangri-la be kept open to visitors. It's on NC-86, east of Hightowers.

Henry Warren's Shangri-la

Catawba

Conover

North Carolina History in Jade

Richard Sipe loves rock. He has spent his working life as a rock mason. His hobby? He's a rockhound, of course.

On a rock hunt in 1972, when he was forty-four years old, Richard dug a 7,000-pound mottled green nephrite jade boulder out of a North Carolina mountainside.

His first plan, once he got his monstrous find home, was simply to polish it and mount it on a pedestal next to his house.

In 1976, moved by the nation's bicentennial celebration, Richard decided to carve America's history into his boulder. A friend suggested that maybe he was being a little overly ambitious and should restrict himself to North Carolina's history. Richard agreed and began chipping away at his boulder with air-impact chisels.

Next to his house, he erected a heated and lighted teepeelike tent over the boulder so he could work on it at night and in bad weather, and he's worked thousands of hours so far. His plan is to show the state's history along a road that begins in a tunnel of the distant past and winds around the rock into the infinity of the future.

Although he's never attempted sculpture before, Richard thinks he has a knack for it. "I have a pretty good eye," he says. "The rock dictates to me."

After suffering nerve damage from a fall in 1987, Richard had to give up working on his project, but he hopes to recover enough to return to it. Meanwhile he invites visitors to see what he has accomplished so far. The sculpture is on display in his yard on County Home Road, three miles from NC-16. For an appointment, call (704) 464-0597.

Hickory

World's Largest Arrowhead Collection

In 1940, Moon Mullins went to Georgia on vacation and found seven arrowheads. His wife, Irene, suggested collecting arrowheads might be a fun hobby.

Moon Mullins stands outside his museum, which houses the world's largest collection of arrowheads

"We started huntin' and we started buildin' and buildin' and buildin'," says Moon. "It's something got in me that I don't know. It'll grow on you and it'll hit you like that."

Through twenty states Moon and Irene hunted arrowheads – and they always found them.

"When I started this collection, if you'd told me, 'Moon, did you know that one day you'd have the largest collection of Indian arrowheads in the world?' I'd have said you were crazy. And now look at it. And I'm not braggin'. I don't know of anybody I would say as an individual in the world who has as big a collection as mine."

The collection numbers nearly half a million pieces, not only arrowheads but axes, tomahawks, hammers, stunners, spearheads, knives, fishhooks, gigs, needles, pestles, celts, pipes, idols, and good luck charms, some dating back 20,000 years.

Over the years more than half a million people have come to see Moon's collection in an old building behind his house at 1228 Second Street, just off US-64 in Hickory. The building also houses a sixty-four-seat movie theater with four professional projectors and a large collection of old movies.

Moon died in 1987, but he left his arrowhead museum and theater to his friend Jerry Williams, who shows it to visitors by appointment at no charge. Call (704) 327-5921.

Bernard's Waldensian Winery Museum

Waldensians who came to western North Carolina from Italy brought with them a tradition of wine making. About 1930, Mallie C. Bernard, who died in 1980, opened a commercial Waldensian winery in Icard, a Burke County town near the Caldwell County line.

A success from the beginning, the winery made popular wines from apples, peaches, strawberries, and other fruits, as well as from native grapes. But its best seller was pokeberry, touted as a cure for rheumatism.

In 1948, Burke County voted against alcohol sales and forced the winery to close. More than 66,000 gallons of wine had to be turned to vinegar.

For the next thirty-five years, the winery and all its equipment sat idle. But in the fall of 1983, Mallie J. Bernard, who grew up working in his father's winery, joined with Leonard Bumgarner and Lorin Weaver to open Bernard's Waldensian Winery Museum in Hickory.

The museum includes much of the old equipment, including grape crushers, presses, and 1,000-gallon redwood aging casks. The three men also revived Bernard's Waldensian Wines, having them made to old recipes under contract by another North Carolina winery, and these wines are available for tasting in the museum. The new wines will include mountain huckleberry and sourwood honey, but there are no plans for reviving the once popular pokeberry.

The museum is in Kathryn's Cheese House on US-64 West, just a few miles from the winery's original location in nearby Icard. It is open 10:00 A.M.-6:00 P.M., daily, without charge. For more information, call (704) 327-2743.

Chatham

Bonsal

North Carolina Railway Museum

In 1982, the East Carolina Chapter of the National Railway Historical Society raised $48,000 to buy a 6-mile abandoned railroad spur near B. Everett Jordan Lake from Southern Railway.

To this spur, the club moved two locomotives, two flat cars, two boxcars, an old postal car, two old cabooses, and several hand cars given to it over the years by different railroad companies. Restored by members, this equipment forms the nucleus of the New Hope Valley Railway, named for the original line that ran over the tracks from Bonsal to Durham.

This line, functioning only for the benefit of visitors, will be the centerpiece of the North Carolina Railway Museum the club plans to build in Bonsal as soon as money is available.

The equipment, meanwhile, can be seen on the tracks at Bonsal on State Road 1008.

Bynum

World's Largest Stump and Root Zoo

Clyde Jones had his leg crushed by a log while working on a pulp-wood crew in 1981. During his recovery, a friend stopped by to visit. In the back of his friend's pickup truck was the gnarled and weathered stump of a cedar tree. Clyde thought he saw something in the stump and asked if he could have it. His friend gave it to him, and with a few strokes of a chainsaw, Clyde revealed what he'd seen in the stump: a goat.

He put the goat on display in the front yard of his three-room house on Thompson Recreation Street, and went looking for other stumps and roots that he could turn into animals. Within five years, he had turned his entire yard – front, back, and sides – into a stump and root zoo crowded with every conceivable creature – elephants, pigs, deer, moose, snakes, dolphins, birds, sheep, cows, gorillas, and some that only Clyde can see – many of them painted in bright colors. As word of his zoo spread, Clyde picked up a new nickname, Jungle Boy, which he heralded with a big sign in his yard.

Some experts have proclaimed Clyde's creatures art and Clyde an artist. He doesn't know whether that's so or not.

"I just think of myself as doing the things I like," he says. "It's what I love to do. I'm trying things. That's all a man can do is try, you know."

Siler City

Milo Holt's Memory Mobile

It's a small trailer painted green. Milo Holt calls it his memory mobile. Inside, Bob Steele, Ken Maynard, Hoot Gibson, and all the old movie cowboys still ride the range.

When Milo was growing up, those old cowboys reigned every Saturday at the Gem Theater in Siler City.

"We'd make a dime somehow and go to the show and spend Saturday afternoon watching the old cowboys," he remembers. "This was our biggest thrill for a whole week."

Milo never got over that thrill. He loved the old cowboys and even as a boy he collected photos of them and posters of their movies. Then in the mid-1950s, when the old cowboy movies died out, he began renting films and showing them at home to friends. That led to collecting films along with other memorabilia.

When the collection got to be too much for his house in 1970, Milo bought the old trailer and filled it. There several times a week and frequently on weekends he shows old cowboy movies to visitors and lets them view his collection, which includes a saddle once owned by silent movie star Fred Thompson.

In addition to the showings at the Memory Mobile, Milo regularly organizes larger gatherings of old cowboy movie buffs.

The Memory Mobile is about 5 miles east of Siler City on US-64 at Collins Pond. Cross the dam and turn right onto Memory Lane. Milo has no phone but is usually available nights and weekends.

Aunt Bee's House

Francis Bavier, a New York actress, appeared in movies and plays for twenty-two years without achieving great fame until 1960, when she landed a role as Aunt Bee in "The Andy Griffith Show" on CBS.

The show became number one in the ratings and won Frances Bavier an Emmy before it ended in 1970. It remains a top-rated rerun show.

In 1963, Francis Bavier came to North Carolina to undergo the famous rice diet at Duke University. While there she became friends with a Siler City woman who invited her to her home and took her on a tour around the state. It was Miss Bavier who urged "The Andy Griffith Show" writers to work Siler City into the story line of the show, which was set in North Carolina.

After her retirement from show business in 1972, Miss Bavier bought a large stone and brick house at 503 West Elk Street in Siler City and settled there. In her early years in the town, she made frequent public appearances in the area, but after her health began to fail, she went into seclusion.

Devil's Tramping Ground

It has been there for hundreds of years, a circular path in the woods, 40 feet in diameter, barren of growth.

It is one of North Carolina's best-known mysteries. Legend holds it is the place where the devil comes to tramp and brood and conjure evil in the darkness of night. Over the years, thousands of people have spent a scary night at the site, hoping to catch the devil at work. In the process, they have chopped down most of the trees for firewood and littered the privately owned site to the point of transforming it into a dump.

At one time the site was marked with a sign and even sported a picnic table for visitors, but vandals destroyed them.

Scientific tests have proved that soil in the mysterious path is sterile, although the reason is unknown.

The Devil's Tramping Ground is about 10 miles south of Siler City on State Road 1100, about one mile north of NC-902 at Harper's Crossroads. A gravel pull-off beside the road marks the site.

Cleveland

Shelby

The B King

It could be any other industrial complex. A low, white office building by the road, big warehouses down the hill, a sign that says "The EO Corp." The only indication that this might be something other than a typical industrial plant is a big chalet behind the office with a statuary-lined pool, airstrip, and garage with Rolls-Royce and airplane.

The chalet is home to movie mogul Earl Owensby, who has been

called "the Cecil B. DeMille of the South" and "King of the Bs."
The other buildings on the 112 rolling acres around the house
make up the most efficient movie studio in the world, Earl
Owensby likes to proclaim.

Earl Owensby was given away as a baby to a couple who later
adopted him. He grew up in Cliffside, a small mill town in
Rutherford County, where as a boy and young man he delivered
newspapers and worked in the town movie theater and a cannery.
He joined the Marines, later became a tool salesman, and eventually
started his own tool company in Shelby.

But movies intrigued him – he is a devoted fan of *Gone With the
Wind* – and in 1973 he decided to make one, strictly as a business
venture.

"This was the only business the South didn't really have," he
says. "It was just economics. It just had to work."

Owensby put a few hundred thousand dollars into an action- and
violence-packed film called *Challenge* – starring Earl Owensby. It
brought in $3 million, and Owensby decided he had found the
right business and began building his studio.

The studio includes complete production facilities, with 100,000
square feet of soundproof studio space, underwater filming
facilities, and the largest cyclorama stage in the world. Here
Owensby has turned out, among many others, such movies as
Death Driver, Wolfman, Living Legend, and *Buckstone County Prison* –
all starring Earl Owensby. None of his movies has ever lost money.

"There's nothing artistic about our movies," he admits. "They're
commercial, you know, strictly commercial."

Independent producers have used the studio to make films that
are more than commercial, though; one of them was the highly
acclaimed *Reuben, Reuben.*

The studio, which is on Old Boiling Springs Road, off US-74
and NC-150, offers tours on a limited group basis by appointment
only, but never while films are in production. Call (704) 482-0611.

Home of the Man Whose Book Became
the First Classic Movie

Thomas Dixon was born near Shelby on January 11, 1864, and
grew up in the town. After studying law at Wake Forest College,
he returned home and was elected to the legislature. He resigned to
become a Baptist preacher but left that calling to write novels and
melodramatic plays. His novel, *The Clansman*, published in 1905,

was made into the first classic film, *Birth of a Nation*, by his friend
D.W. Griffith. Dixon died in Raleigh on April 3, 1946. Dixon's
family home on Marion Street has been demolished, but the site,
now a vacant lot, is marked by a historical plaque.

Davidson

Churchland

Daniel Boone's Cave

Daniel Boone, the great frontiersman who cut the Wilderness Trail
across the mountains into Tennessee and Kentucky, supposedly hid
from Indians in a cave on a high hill overlooking the Yadkin River.
The cave, with a two-foot opening and a ceiling height ranging
from three to five feet, measures about 45 by 80 feet. It and 110
acres surrounding it are owned by the state and used as a park. A
cabin where Boone once lived has been restored on the site.

The cave is off NC-150 on State Road 1167, reachable by State
Roads 1165 and 1162.

Boone's parents, Squire and Sarah Boone, are buried in Joppa
Cemetery on NC-601, a mile northwest of Mocksville in
neighboring Davie County.

Denton

Denton International Airport Fly-In, Old-Time Threshers Convention, And Brown Loflin's Handy Dandy Railroad

As a boy, Brown Loflin would sit in school watching out the
window, enthralled as the steam locomotive made its regular run
through Denton.

A born tinkerer, Brown was fascinated by anything mechanical.
He was breaking down and rebuilding gasoline engines before
he was ten. By seventeen, he was flying airplanes and building
racing cars.

After prospering in business, Brown bought an 80-acre farm
south of Denton and built a grass airstrip on it. In 1970, he and
some other pilots gave airplane rides on the July 4th weekend
to raise money for the rescue squad. The event was so successful

that it was held again the next summer, and the next. So many people came that the rescue squad started selling hot dogs and hamburgers.

"Somebody said, 'We ought to have an ol' timey wheat threshing dinner,'" Brown recalls. "I said, 'Why don't we just have a wheat threshing?'"

The next year, he bought and rebuilt an old steam threshing machine and the wheat threshing was added to the airplane rides. More steam devices came the following year and people began bringing their own steam engines to show off. Within a few years, the event had become the biggest steam show in the South. A steam sawmill, rock crusher, giant steam shovel, steamroller, even a functioning moonshine still were added to the show. In 1979, Brown bought his ultimate steam machine, a fifty-ton H.K. Porter locomotive. By 1982, he had it restored and puffing around more than a mile of track laid out around the perimeter of his farm.

In addition to the steam devices, large numbers of antique gasoline and alcohol engines are displayed, powering everything from grist mills to clocks. The world's smallest steam-operated sawmill also can be seen.

The event lasts four days every July 4th weekend and includes music, dancing, military encampments and battle reenactments, skydiving shows, and a huge flea market. Admission is charged. Brown's farm is off NC-49 south of Denton. Signs mark the way. His Handy Dandy Railroad also operates on some other occasions during the year. For more information, call him at (704) 869-3663.

Lexington

Barbecue Center of the Universe

It started in the twenties with tents pitched on a vacant lot across from the courthouse and pork shoulders cooking slowly over hickory coals in improvised cinder-block pits. Sid Weaver and Varner Swicegood competed to sell barbecue trays and sandwiches to the crowds who came on court days.

That was the beginning of a whole school of North Carolina barbecueing, now called Lexington-style, which became the dominant barbecue of the state's Piedmont.

North Carolina evolved two primary schools of barbecue: Eastern, in which whole pigs are cooked and served with white or yellow slaw, and Lexington, in which only shoulders are cooked and served with red slaw.

While Eastern barbecuers have largely turned to gas and electricity to cook their so-called barbecue, Lexington barbecuers have clung to tradition, cooking only over hickory coals, as barbecue was meant to be cooked.

The tents across from the courthouse eventually became buildings. Warner Stamey bought out Varner Swicegood and spread Lexington barbecue to Greensboro. Sid Weaver was bought out by Allen Beck. Men who worked for Stamey and Beck went out on their own, opening barbecue houses in other nearby towns. But many remained in Lexington, and remarkably, the town has managed to support them. Lexington has more barbecue houses per capita than any place known – sixteen for a population of about 16,000 – and all cook with wood.

They have made Lexington famous with barbecue fanciers, and that fame has spread worldwide. Lexington barbecuer Wayne Monk of Lexington Barbecue #1 was summoned to cook for international leaders at the Williamsburg Summit Conference in 1983.

In 1984, Lexington began holding an annual Barbecue Festival on the third weekend of October. Barbecue is served on the town square and a parade of pigs is held. More than 50,000 people attend every year.

Original Golden Berry Holly

It was just a freak of nature, a holly tree that sprouted yellow berries instead of red. Matthew Morgan found it growing in a pasture on his father's farm in Rowan County and moved it to his front yard in Lexington at 20 Morgan Drive. That was where Minnie Darr, a local holly enthusiast, saw it.

Minnie took clippings from the tree to a Holly Society of America convention in 1959 and created a sensation. Officially registered as a new variety of holly, the Morgan Gold, the tree gained worldwide fame. Offspring from it, created by grafting cuttings from the tree, grow in the National Arboretum and in Britain's Royal Gardens.

Thomasville

World's Largest Duncan Phyfe Chair

One day in 1921, Charles Sturkey, managing editor of the weekly *Chair Town News*, got to boasting to a fellow newspaperman from another town about how many chairs were made in Thomasville's several furniture factories. He pointed out that enough chairs were produced in the town to allow every resident to sit in a new one every day. In his enthusiasm, he got carried away and went on to tell how Thomasville was going to build the largest chair in the world to note its eminence in chair building.

There was no such plan, and the editor was taken aback a few days later when a story about the big chair appeared in his friend's newspaper and requests for more information began coming in.

To save face, Sturkey talked the town fathers into building such a chair and in 1922, Thomasville Chair Co. (later to become Thomasville Furniture Industries) assigned four men to the task.

The chair was built at the company's Plant C and contained enough lumber to build one hundred ordinary dining-room chairs.

"We made it out of forest pine," one of the workers, Walter Loftin, would recall years later, "the best wood we had. We had to build it in what was the bending room, because that was the only department which had a big enough door so we could get the chair out."

The chair was 13.5 feet tall and was upholstered with leather from the hide of a single Swiss steer. It was erected in the heart of town alongside the mainline Southern Railway tracks so passengers in passing trains could see it.

Gradually, the chair decayed and in the mid-1930s it was dismantled. But people in town had grown accustomed to the big chair and they kept talking about what a shame it was that they didn't have it any more.

Finally, in 1948, the Chamber of Commerce and the chair company agreed to build a new one that would last. The Duncan Phyfe design was chosen and local sculptor James Harvey set about building the chair of steel and concrete. The 12-foot-tall limestone base was anchored 8 feet deep. The chair rose 18 feet above the base, and solid brass rods were used in its lyre back.

Dedicated in 1951, the chair remains the town's centerpiece at the corner of Randolph and Main streets. Several Misses America and President Lyndon B. Johnson have climbed into the chair to pose for pictures.

World's largest Duncan Phyfe chair

Durham

Durham

Pharmacy Museum

Elsie Booker is a pharmacist who is fascinated by old things. Soon
after her graduation from pharmacy school in 1945, she did
some relief work in old-time drug stores and became intrigued
with some of the old tonics and potions she saw on the shelves.
She started collecting them.

Her husband, John, a tobacco company employee, collected
tobacco paraphernalia, and together they began scouring the
country, adding to their collections. In the process, they picked up
a lot of other items from old stores, and in 1973 they decided to
make use of them by opening Patterson's Mill Country Store on
Farrington Road, off NC-54 between Raleigh, Durham, and
Chapel Hill. The store is a replica of an old-time store, furnished
with what has been described as one of the nation's best collections
of mercantile Americana. It offers North Carolina hand-crafted
items for sale.

In 1974, the Bookers built a wing onto the store to house Elsie's
extensive collection of old-time pharmaceuticals and pharmacy
equipment, including more than 10,000 patent medicines, pills,
tonics, and potions, some dating back to 1880. The wing is a
replica of a turn-of-the-century pharmacy. Adjoining it is an old-
time doctor's office. Visitors may browse through both at no charge.

Elsie's collection has been recognized by the American Institute
of the History of Pharmacy, as well as by the Smithsonian
Institution, as one of America's finest.

"Smithsonian says it far surpasses theirs," says Elsie.

The store is open Monday-Saturday, 10:00 A.M.-5:30 P.M.; Sunday, 2:00-5:30 P.M. For more information, call (919) 493-8149.

Dinosaurs Alive!

Each year in January and February, the North Carolina Museum
of Life and Science presents "Dinosaurs Alive!," an exhibit of
animated dinosaurs, one-third their original sizes. Exhibited in
natural settings, the dinosaurs move and roar realistically. Among
those shown are triceratops, stegosaurus, brontosaurus,

Tyrannosaurus rex, and the flying pteranodon. The traveling dinosaurs, built by a California company at an average cost of $60,000 each, are the museum's most popular exhibit, drawing nearly 100,000 visitors annually. The show also includes dinosaur art, films, and lectures. The museum at 433 Murray Avenue is open Monday-Saturday, 10:00 A.M.-5:00 P.M., and Sunday, 1:00-5:00 P.M. Admission is charged.

The Tobacco Museum

At the end of the Civil War, an Orange County tobacco farmer named Washington Duke walked home from the war to find that most of his goods had been pilfered except for a 25-pound sack of tobacco he had carefully hidden.

He toasted the tobacco, spread it over a corncrib floor, and then, together with his three sons, beat it with sticks until it was shredded enough to be smoked. This he packaged and sold. Thus was the beginning of the world's largest tobacco company.

Soon Duke began processing tobacco in an old barn. Then he built a two-story factory, one room upstairs, one down, near his house. By 1874, W. Duke & Sons Tobacco Co. had moved into downtown Durham to compete against the W.T. Blackwell Tobacco Co., makers of the popular Bull Durham Tobacco.

Ten years later, a cigarette machine was perfected and Duke managed to get sole rights to it. With these machines, Washington Duke's youngest son, James Buchanan, went to New York and started a factory that soon gobbled up all the other major tobacco companies. From 1890 to 1911 when the government forced its breakup, Duke's American Tobacco Company was the world's largest.

James Buchanan Duke went on to become a tycoon, moving into aluminum, railroads, textiles, and electrical power (he founded Duke Power Co.). In 1924, he gave $40 million to Trinity College to establish Duke University.

The old Duke homestead was owned by the university until 1974, when it was given to the state. Three years later, it was opened as a state historic site and tobacco museum. Tobacco equipment and paraphernalia may be seen, along with a twenty-two-minute film detailing the story of tobacco. The house, the corncrib where Duke started his company, and the two-story factory may be toured.

Each year on the last weekend in July, a tobacco barn party is held to demonstrate how tobacco once was tied on sticks and hung in mud-chinked log barns to be cured with wood fires. The party includes roasting corn and making hoecakes in the curing fire ashes.

On the first Sunday in October a mock tobacco auction is held at the museum, featuring professional auctioneers, including the winner of the tobacco autioneering world championships held in Danville, Virginia.

The museum, at 2828 Duke Homestead Road, is open 9:00 A.M.-5:00 P.M. daily, 1:00-5:00 P.M. Sunday, without charge. For more information, call (919) 477-5498.

Corn crib where Washington Duke started world's largest tobacco company, at tobacco museum

World's First Jazz Conservatory

Thelonious Monk, gifted jazz pianist and composer of "Round Midnight" and many other songs, was born in Rocky Mount but moved to New York as a child. He died in 1982 at age sixty-four.

After his death, his son, T. S. Monk, also a jazz musician, decided that his father should be honored by the building of a conservatory to teach jazz musicians and scholars, the first of its kind. He chose Durham for its location. Such well-known figures as Bill Cosby, Clint Eastwood, Steve Allen, Kareem Abdul Jabar, Quincy Jones, and Senator Bob Dole have joined to raise $72 million to build and fund the conservatory, which will be housed in a new $12-million building at the corner of Foster and Morgan streets in downtown Durham.

Leading jazz musicians and educators will teach at the conservatory, which will be affiliated with Duke University. If the fundraising drive is successful, students will attend tuition-free. The conservatory, which will accommodate about 150 students, is scheduled to open in 1991.

World's First University Parapsychology Lab

In 1927, a botanist named Joseph B. Rhine, who had become interested in psychic phenomena, set up the first university research program into the paranormal in the psychology department of Duke University.

Rhine's experiments with clairvoyance and telepathy made him the leading authority on psychic phenomena and brought him great fame, although his findings were often disputed by other scientists. Rhine wrote several books about parapsychology, including *New Frontiers of the Mind*, which became a best seller and Book of the Month Club selection in 1937.

Despite controversy about his techniques and findings, Rhine continued his work at Duke for nearly forty years. After his retirement from the university, he established the Foundation for Research on the Nature of Man at 402 North Buchanan Boulevard. Rhine died in 1980 at age eighty-four, but the foundation continues his work.

Forsyth

Clemmons

North Carolina Chili Championship

North Carolina may be barbecue heaven, but it also harbors its share of chiliheads and hundreds of them turn out on the third Saturday in August for the state chili championship cookoff at Tanglewood Park, sponsored by the March of Dimes. Participants compete not only for taste and heat but for show. Cooks use many secret ingredients, and mystery meats range from possum to venison. Among the names cooks have given their chilis are Hot Rise, Demon's Fare, Canyon Fire, Genuine Blue Flame, Firehouse Red, Mountain Heat, Twelve Volt, Firestarter, Red Death, Snake Bite, and the ever popular Thunder Bottom.

Kernsville

Korner's Folly

Jule Korner was the grandson of Joseph Korner, who founded Kernersville. With his inheritance he invested successfully in real estate, allowing him time to pursue his other interests, art and interior decorating. But it was his genius for advertising that brought him fame.

Using the name Ruben Rink, Korner made Bull Durham tobacco world famous in the last century. He created and painted the roll-your-own tobacco's bull symbol on barns across the nation and even on the Rock of Gibraltar and the pyramids of Egypt. His fortune amassed, he returned to Kernersville to design and build his dream house, an ornate, eclectic house of twenty-two rooms on seven levels. A passing farmer, observing the construction of the peculiar house, was heard to remark, "That will surely be Jules Korner's Folly." Hearing of it, Korner had "Korner's Folly" inlaid in tile across the main entrance.

Korner was a bachelor when he started the house in 1878. He expanded and remodeled it eight years later when he married. The house includes a ballroom with statuary and ornate wood carvings. An upper floor offers a little theater with murals and frescoes on the ceiling. On the front porch is a small fireplace called "The Witches

Corner," provided to keep witches out of the house. One room in the home was designed to be fireproof. Built of tile and marble, it was called the smoker and was the only room in the house where Korner, a nontobacco user, allowed smoking.

Korner's Folly remained in the Korner family until it was bought and restored by a nonprofit foundation in 1970. It is open Sundays, 1:00-5:00 P.M., for a fee. For information, call Kernersville's Chamber of Commerce (919) 993-4521.

Winston-Salem

The Last Shell Station

When the owners of Quality Oil Co., local distributors of Shell Oil products, began looking for a way to promote business, they came up with the idea of building gas stations in the shape of a seashell. In 1930, they built eight such stations, constructing the form of wire and plastering it with concrete. The stations fulfilled their purpose, attracting national attention. Now only one remains, at the corner of Sprague and Peachtree streets in Winston-Salem. The structure, no longer used, is the only individual gas station included in the National Register of Historic Places.

North Carolina Storytellers Convention

North Carolina has an oral tradition that allows it to support more than a dozen full-time storytellers and scores more who tell stories just for fun or part-time profit, and each year on the first weekend in May they gather in Winston-Salem to conduct workshops and practice their art.

Folk tales, fairy tales, tall tales, legends – all kinds of stories – can be heard at the concert that is part of the North Carolina Storytellers Convention. And you don't have to be a professional to participate. Anybody who has a story to tell can tell it – with certain restrictions.

"Most people will respect themselves and not get up and tell those little nasty stories," says Shirley Holloway, a full-time storyteller and founder and director of the Tar Heel Association of Storytellers, which sponsors the convention. "Of course," she adds with a chuckle, "when we're by ourselves we tell those stories."

The convention is held at different sites in and around Winston-

Salem and a fee is charged. For more information, write Shirley
Holloway at 818 Woodcote St., Winston-Salem, 27107, or call
(919) 788-8948.

World's Biggest Defunct Windmill

When it was dedicated atop Howard's Knob near Boone in 1979,
it gave great hope.

It was the world's largest windmill, a response to the energy
crisis, a joint project of NASA and the federal Department of
Energy. It had been built at a cost of $3.5 million, and its two huge
blades, spanning 210 feet, running at a speed of 25 m.p.h. were
supposed to generate enough energy to power 500 homes.

But there were problems from the day the blades first started
turning. Nearby residents complained that the windmill not only
interfered with their TV reception but created an infernal racket
that couldn't be tolerated.

By the time the windmill broke down for the last time in 1981,
much to the relief of nearby residents, the federal government had
spent more than $30 million trying to keep it running.

The windmill was disassembled in 1983 and the huge blades
were donated to the Nature Science Center in Winston-Salem
where they now stand mounted on Hanes Mill Road as the center's
sign.

World's Second Largest Painting

In 1880, French historical artist Paul Philippoteaux, painter of
many cycloramas, came to the United States to undertake what he
called "the greatest effort of my life" – a cyclorama of the climax
of the Civil War Battle of Gettysburg on July 3, 1863.

It took Philippoteaux and sixteen assistants two and a half years
to finish it. The painting was put on display in Chicago in 1883
and in the first year attracted nearly half a million people, who paid
nearly $250,000 to see it.

The painting eventually passed into the hands of Emmett
McConnell of Hollywood, who owned and exhibited many such
cycloramas. He last exhibited it in 1932. For the next thirty years,
the painting remained stored in a Chicago warehouse.

In 1964, Winston-Salem painter Joe King, who was commis-
sioned to do portraits of President Richard Nixon, Queen Eliza-

beth, and the royalty of Saudi Arabia, bought the painting as a curiosity. Since then he has kept it in a warehouse in Winston-Salem, unavailable to the public.

Joe says he would like to change that and put the painting on view. It would take quite a building to display it. The painting is 70 feet tall – the height of a seven-story building – and 410 feet long. It weighs 12,000 pounds.

World's Largest Coffee Pot

When customers complained to Julius Mickey that they had trouble finding the tin shop he and his brother Samuel operated on Main Street in Salem, an early Moravian community, Julius was quoted as saying, "I'll put up a sign that will tell everybody where I am and where I do business."

That he did. On a pole in front of his shop, he and his brother built a coffee pot 16 feet in circumference and more than 12 feet tall. That was in 1858.

Why the brothers chose a coffee pot for a symbol isn't known, but coffee pots were considered necessities in those days and the tin shop was across the street from a public camping ground and coffee pots dangled from the sides of all the wagons of travelers who gathered there.

No matter why they chose it, the coffee pot was a success. Its fame spread widely, and eventually it became a symbol for Salem itself.

It stood in the same spot for a century, but construction of Interstate 40 caused it to be moved, first to a temporary location, later to its present spot on the north side of the Old Salem restoration at Main Street and the Salem bypass.

Franklin

Louisburg

National Whistling Convention And World's Largest Collection of Recorded Whistling Music

In 1974 at a folk festival on the campus of Louisburg College, a singer decided to whistle his tune instead of sing it. The crowd loved it, and at the next year's festival a small whistling contest was held under a big oak tree on the campus.

The contest grew every year until the folk festival was overwhelmed and forgotten. By 1981, the contest had become the National Whistling Convention, bringing some of the world's most famous whistlers to Franklin County Courthouse on the third weekend each April.

Professional whistlers perform concerts of popular and classical music, but the highlight of the day is the whistling contest. Competitors come from all over the country and employ many whistling styles. There are pucker whistlers, teeth whistlers, tongue whistlers, and finger whistlers of many varieties.

Awards are given for youngest and oldest whistler, for popular music and classical, for special sounds and loud whistling (111 decibels took the award in 1983), and a national champion whistler is named.

During the convention, the National Whistling Museum is open in an old store building across from the courthouse. The museum houses whistling memorabilia and the world's largest collection of recorded whistling music. During the convention, the museum also displays the world's largest collection of whistles, owned by Carlin N. Morton of Ft. Myers Beach, Florida. The museum may be seen by appointment throughout the year. For information about the museum or the convention, write Allen de Hart, Franklin County Arts Council, P.O. Box 758, Louisburg, NC 27549, or call (919) 496-2521.

Where the First Confederate Flag Was Unfurled

Major Orren Randolph Smith had fought in the Mexican War and served in the U.S. Army under General Zachary Taylor before the looming conflict between the states over slavery caused him to resign his commission and return home to Franklin County to lead the fight for secession. Realizing that the cause of the southern states needed a flag to rally around, he designed one in February 1861, and asked his friend Becky Murphy, a young widow, to make it for him from silk dress goods that he bought from Barrow's Store in Louisburg.

The tiny flag was similar to the stars and stripes of the Union. It featured a circle of seven white stars on a field of blue with three broad stripes, one white between two red. The stars represented the seven states that had already seceded. The stripes represented

church, state, and press; the white color stood for purity, the blue
for constancy, the red for defiance. Major Smith sent his flag to the
Confederate capital in Montgomery, Alabama, where it was
adopted by the Congress on March 4.

Learning of its adoption, Major Smith had Becky Murphy make
a large copy of it, 9 feet by 12. She later recalled that she sewed it
while her sister Sarah, an ardent Unionist, entertained her Yankee
officer boyfriend (whom she later married) in the next room by
playing "Yankee Doodle Dandy" on the piano.

On March 18, 1861, Major Smith, waving his flag, led a march
around the Franklin County Courthouse in Louisburg, where most
people had been opposed to secession. With great ceremony, amidst
much whooping, he raised his flag on a tall pole made from two
freshly cut poplar trees erected on a corner of the courthouse square.
The event turned into a rallying of volunteers to fight for the
Confederacy.

In a speech that proved to be less than prophetic, Furney Green,
a local planter who later led the Franklin County Rifles, urged
the men to join the fight. "We'll whip them out before breakfast,"
he cried, "and I'll wipe up all the blood spilt with my pocket
handkerchief."

Four years later, when General Sherman's victorious troops
marched into Louisburg, they cut down the pole upon which the
first Confederate flag was flown, moved it to another corner of the
courthouse square, and raised the stars and stripes of the Union
on it.

Actually, Major Smith's flag flew over the Confederacy for only
two years, until it was replaced by a new design, which was
replaced by yet another design before the Confederacy crumbled.
The flag now commonly called the Confederate flag – a blue St.
Andrews cross with white stars on a field of red – never was the
official flag of the Confederate states but only a battle flag used by
the army to distinguish its forces from those of the Union.

In 1935, the Alabama legislature claimed that the first Confederate flag was designed by a Montgomery artist, Nicola Marschall.
Some historians think it possible that two similar designs were
submitted simultaneously, but in 1915 the Confederate Veterans,
meeting in Richmond, decreed that Major Smith was the designer
of the first flag. The United Daughters of the Confederacy also
recognized Smith as the designer and erected a monument to him
and Becky Murphy in front of the Franklin County Courthouse
in downtown Louisburg.

Gaston

Cherryville

America's Only Trucking Museum

When Grier Beam was growing up on a farm near Cherryville,
he was mainly interested in chickens. He loved working with them
but he had to do other farm chores, too, as well as work at his
father's sawmill and cotton gin.

When he went away to college at North Carolina State, he
studied poultry science and got a degree in it in 1931. He immediately landed a job with a poultry co-op in Florida. Soon afterward,
the price of eggs dropped, and the co-op folded.

The Depression was on and Beam was unable to find a job, so he
returned home, bought a used '31 Chevrolet truck for $360 on
credit, and began hauling coal to the county schools and making
regular runs to Florida to bring back oranges and vegetables.

From that small beginning grew Carolina Freight Carriers, the
largest trucking company in North Carolina, and tenth largest
in the nation. It has more than 5,000 employees and hauls freight
all over North America and Europe.

Over the years, Beam kept a lot of the old trucks that his
company phased out and made a hobby of restoring them. But he
was never able to find a '31 Chevrolet like the one he had used
to start his company. When he did finally find one, he decided to
open a trucking museum with it as the featured attraction.

To house his collection of trucks, he built a building on
Mountain Street in Cherryville, next to the old gas station in which
he once had used a corner as his first office. He opened the museum
in the fall of 1982 with fourteen trucks and displays about the
trucking business. The museum, known as the Carolina Freight
Carriers Museum, charges no admission and is open Thursday 1:00-
5:00 P.M., Friday 10:00 A.M.-5:00 P.M., and Saturday 10:00 A.M.-
3:00 P.M. For more information, call (704) 435-3072.

New Year's Shoot-In

On New Year's Day, you might say that Cherryville is a booming
town.

For more than 150 years, townspeople have followed a tradition started by the town's German settlers, who believed that bad luck and witches could be driven away by welcoming a new year with black powder explosions.

On New Year's Day, dozens of residents armed with old muskets and plenty of black powder go from house to house and business to business in the town. At each stop they recite an old sing-song chant designed to bring good luck, then one by one discharge their muskets with resounding booms. The annual ritual usually takes all day to complete. When New Year's Day falls on Sunday, it is held on January 2.

Dellview

America's Smallest Town

At one time every family in Dellview owned a Dodge and the Chrysler Company was so impressed that it wrote a story about the town in its company magazine. Didn't matter that there were only two families in town.

Dellview was incorporated in 1924, so the story goes, because brothers A.T. and J. Henry Dellinger wanted to give themselves authority to shoot stray dogs that threatened their chicken business. Of course, some say it was because Duke Power Company would only extend its lines to incorporated areas.

The town was incorporated in a square of which each side was 1,500 feet long. The only brick structure in town, a chicken incubator, sat at its exact center.

At one point, deaths brought the town's population down to one, Mrs. J. Henry Dellinger, who elected herself mayor and town board and then named herself police chief, but by the 1980 census, population had risen to eight. Dellview is on NC-150 on the western edge of Cherryville.

Gastonia

Fish Camp Festival

Two rivers merge in Gaston County, and along those rivers in the early part of this century fish camps sprang up, often just crude shacks or even tents where people gathered to cook their catches or to offer fried catfish, frogs' legs, and turtle steaks to passersby.

Some of these places evolved into large restaurants that now attract huge crowds especially on Friday and Saturday nights, but they are still called fish camps, and there are more than twenty in Gaston County.

"We consider ourselves the fish camp capital of the world," says Leanne Webb.

As a child growing up in neighboring South Carolina, Leanne came to the fish camps to eat with her family almost every week, so when she became director of the Gaston County United Arts Council and began looking for a festival to bring the community together, the fish camps naturally came to mind.

Thus was born the Fish Camp Festival, held on the Saturday of the third full week in October each year. Fried fish and other sea-foods are sold and entertainment is provided on five stages.

Highlight of the event: the catfish races, held in water-filled troughs. Hundreds of fish compete. "And, of course, they all have names," says Leanne, "such as Leonardo Da Fishi." Call (704) 922-9938.

McAdenville

Christmas Town

In 1956, the McAdenville Men's Club decorated some trees around the town's community center for Christmas. They used red, green, and white lights, and the reception was so good that they decorated a few more trees the next year.

Now the town decorates some 250 trees with more than 300,000 lights. A lake in the center of town serves as a reflecting pool for seventy-five of the trees, and colored lights also play on a fountain in the lake.

Decorating of the town begins in September. In addition to the lighted trees, homes in the town are decorated elaborately. A tradition yule log parade is held, and a 30-foot bell tower chimes carols for visitors nightly.

There are visitors aplenty. Nearly a quarter million vehicles pass through the town in December bringing people to see the decorations. The lights glow Monday-Friday, 5:00-9:00 P.M.; Saturday and Sunday, 5:00-10:00 P.M., December 2-26.

Guilford

Greensboro

African Heritage Museum

Mattye Reed spent twelve years in Africa while her husband, William, was a diplomat for the Agency for International Development. During that time, she collected hundreds of African art objects. After she and her husband returned to this country and her husband became director of international affairs at predominantly black A&T State University, Mrs. Reed donated her collection to the African Heritage Center students had started on the campus in the late sixties.

She cleaned and refurbished a campus house to display the collection and opened it as the African Heritage Museum in 1974. Since then, several major African collections have been donated to the museum, which now features more than 3,000 items from twenty-two African nations and the Caribbean. Included are fabrics, baskets, carvings, books, busts of African kings and queens, weapons, ceremonial drums, masks, and many other items. The collection is recognized as one of the nation's finest exhibits of African art. The museum, on Nocho Street on the A&T campus, is open 9:00 A.M.-5:00 P.M., Monday-Friday, at no charge. Weekend tours may be arranged by calling Mattye Reed at (919) 379-7874.

The Curiosities of the Greensboro Historical Museum

O. Henry's Top Hat

William Sydney Porter was born in Guilford County in 1862 and grew up in Greensboro. Shy and artistic, he worked as a teenager at his uncle's drugstore on North Elm Street. At nineteen, he left for adventure in Texas, and there he lived for the next sixteen years, trying his hand at the newspaper business, marrying, fathering a daughter, and finally going to prison for misusing funds while working as a bank teller.

He began writing short stories while in prison, signing them O. Henry. His wife died during his imprisonment, and after his release, he moved to New York with his daughter, Margaret, and gained great fame for his short stories, many of which had surprise endings. Porter's own ending came as no surprise. He died at forty-eight of alcoholism in a lonely New York room strewn with empty liquor bottles.

A replica of Porter's Drugstore, where young Will worked, has been constructed at the Greensboro Historical Museum, furnished with fixtures and equipment from the original drugstore. A replica of the small school he attended as a child, operated by his aunt, Miss Lina Porter, also may be seen.

Other O. Henry exhibits include his cradle, his top hat, letters to his editor, wife, and daughter, the original manuscript pages of one of his stories, and several of his boyhood sketches.

Dolley Madison's Turbans

Dolley Madison was one of this country's most famous first ladies. Wife of James Madison, father of the Constitution and fourth President of the United States, Dolley, who was born in a log cabin near Guilford College, became a national fashion setter as first lady. When she donned a turban hat, fashionable women throughout the country did likewise.

Perhaps none of Dolley's fashions would have survived had it not been for Charles Hafner. In 1956, he was hired by a lawyer to clean up a filthy, refuse-filled house that had been occupied by an eccentric and reclusive widow who had recently died. The woman's husband had been a great-grandson of a niece of James and Dolley Madison. Amidst the garbage, Hafner discovered a trunk that contained not only many of Dolley's fashions, including gowns, capes, turban hats, and slippers, but the Madison family Bible, photographs, and other documents as well.

In 1960 a group of Greensboro citizens raised $10,000 to buy these items, which were then presented to the Greensboro Historical Museum. The fashions and other items are displayed in the Dolley Madison Room.

World's Largest Collection of American Historic Glass

After a family friend who ran an antiques store sold a glass platter commemorating the opening of the West by railroad to Robert McKinney, who ran a Greensboro dry cleaning shop, Robert and his wife, Capelia, got interested in antique glass commemorating American history.

They bought a book on the subject and set out to acquire one of everything described in it. Over the next twenty-five years, they not only accomplished that; they also collected a lot of things that weren't in the book. The result: what is thought to be the biggest and finest collection of antique American historical glass in the world, containing more than 650 rare items, many one of a kind.

Late in 1988, they turned their collection over to the Greensboro Historical Museum, where it was put on permanent display early in 1989. Among the one-of-a-kind items to be seen are a bust of Benjamin Harrison, an elegant 1880 Statue of Liberty compote, a Lincoln-drape syrup pitcher, and a complete set of tableware featuring Jumbo, the famous P.T. Barnum elephant.

The Greensboro Historical Museum is at 130 Summit Avenue. It is open Tuesday-Saturday, 10:00 A.M.-5:00 P.M., Sunday, 2:00-5:00 P.M. There is no admission fee.

Lunch Counter Where Sit-Ins Began

Late in the afternoon of February 1, 1960, four students from Greensboro's all-black North Carolina A&T College – David Richmond, Franklin McCain, Ezell Blair, and Joseph McNeill – walked into the F.W. Woolworth store on South Elm Street and took seats at the lunch counter.

Denied service and asked to leave, they remained seated, prompting the store manager to close the store early. The four left quietly, but the following day a larger group of students appeared and took seats in protest of segregated facilities. Within two months, the sit-ins, as they became called, spread to fifty-four cities in nine states and eventually toppled segregationist policies.

Twenty years later, the four students who started the protests returned to the lunch counter together for the first time since their historic action. This time they came to be honored by the city. They were served breakfast but were unable to eat it because of the attention of so many reporters, photographers, and onlookers.

The lunch counter is still open. F.W. Woolworth's is located at 132 South Elm Street, Greensboro. Their telephone number is (919) 272-8331.

High Point

Angela Peterson's Antique Doll Museum

Angela Peterson lived her first forty-three years in Parkersburg, West Virginia, but she'd always yearned to travel. After the death of her husband in 1945, she decided to do just that.

Over the next thirty-two years, she took a series of teaching jobs, many with the armed forces, that took her all over the world. Her travels led her to begin collecting crèche dolls, some of them hundreds of years old. She collected other dolls as well, and by the time of her retirement in 1977 she had a priceless collection of rare and unique dolls that numbered more than 1,000.

In 1979, she traded the collection to Wesleyan Arms, a retirement center in High Point, in exchange for an apartment for the rest of her life. The Angela Peterson Antique Doll Museum was set up at the First Wesleyan Church at 1915 North Centennial Street so that others could enjoy Angela's collection. The museum is specially decorated at Christmas with Angela's crèche of fifty figures, some dating to the fifteenth century, the central feature.

The museum is free and is open Tuesday through Thursday and on Sunday, 1:30-4:30 P.M., and at other times by appointment. Call (919) 884-1594.

World's Largest Bureau

High Point calls itself the Furniture City and with good reason. Not only is it a center of furniture manufacturing, it is the site of the world's largest furniture show, attracting thousands of furniture store buyers from all over the world each spring and fall.

For more than half a century, the city's symbol of its prominence in the furniture field has been the world's largest bureau. Built in 1926, four years after neighboring Thomasville (which calls itself the Chair City) created the world's biggest chair, the big bureau was designed to share in the publicity Thomasville was attracting. But the bureau also had a practical purpose. It became a visitor center and office for the Chamber of Commerce, which built it.

A frame structure 27 feet long, 14 feet wide, and 32 feet high, the bureau was designed to look as if it had four drawers. A large sign on top gave the appearance of a mirror. The entrance was on the side.

Originally built in Tate Park on North Main Street, the bureau was given to the High Point Jaycees and moved to 508 North Hamilton Street in 1951. The Jaycees installed a basement and later added another room to the back, and the bureau remains the club's offices.

Visitors frequently come to see the bureau and want to look inside. "Particularly children," former Jaycee secretary Katherine Nibbelink was once quoted as saying. "They would come in and ask to see my drawers." For more information, call (919) 883-2016.

World's largest bureau

World's Largest Furniture Library

Nathan Bienenstock, a native of New Rochelle, N.Y., who died at age eighty-six in 1988, began his career as an accountant for *Furniture World*, the nation's oldest furniture publication. He later became the magazine's owner and publisher, bought other furniture publications, and wrote four books about furniture, including *History of American Furniture.*

Not only did he write books about furniture; he also collected them. He spent years traveling the world buying books until he had acquired every significant furniture book published since 1600, the most extensive collection in the world.

In 1970, he bought a granite house at 1009 North Main Street in High Point and transformed it into the Bernice Bienenstock Furniture Library, named for his wife. The library has more than 8,000 volumes, some among the rarest books on earth. It attracts scholars and furniture designers from around the world.

The library is open to the public at no charge. Hours are 9:00 A.M.-noon and 1:00-5:00 P.M., Monday-Friday, other times by appointment. Call (919) 883-4011.

Jamestown

Medieval Festival

The discovery of gold in three places near Jamestown led engineer Charles McCulloch to build a steam-powered gold refinery near the mines in 1832. The big gothic refinery, built of granite around a massive 70-foot-high chimney, operated for thirty years, then fell into ruin. For a century and a quarter it remained a mysterious relic, hidden deep in the woods, attracting curious visitors who thought it a haunted castle.

In 1985, Richard Harris, a machinery designer, bought the ruins and eight acres of land and spent more than two years restoring it. He opened it as a restaurant and club called Castle McCulloch. Each year in May, the club recreates a medieval spring festival with costumed performers, jousting by knights, and a huge feast. Castle McCulloch, which is listed in the National Register of Historic Places, is on Kersey Valley Road. Call (919) 434-3697.

Oak Ridge

Nation's Oldest Continuously Operating Water Mill

It has had many names, most recently Bailes Mill, but generally it has just been called the Old Mill. Built by Nathan Dillon on Beaver Creek about 1745, the mill was captured by British troops before the Battle of Guilford Courthouse during the Revolutionary War.

In 1822 owner Joel Sanders built a larger mill, the current one, downstream from the dam. A succession of owners kept the mill operating with only brief interruptions until 1975, when miller Lloyd Lucas died, making it the oldest water mill in the country in continuous operation. The mill stood idle until 1977, when it was bought by Englishman Charlie Parnell, who still operates it.

"The bloody British are back," Parnell joked after buying it.

Open daily, 6:00 A.M.-9:00 P.M., the mill is located at 1340 NC-68, south of Oak Ridge. For more information, call (919) 643-4783.

Iredell

Barium Springs

Little Joe's Church

In September 1901, a six-year-old boy, Joe Gilland, and his seven-year-old sister, Janie, were brought to Barium Springs Home for Children. The orphanage had no church, and the children had to climb aboard wagons to attend church in the nearby town of Troutman.

Joe didn't care for that travel and announced one day that when he became a man he was going to build a church at the orphanage. A church with a porch. He was adamant about the porch.

Early in the winter of 1904, Joe fell ill and died. Under his pillow was found an old purse with 45 cents in it, pennies he'd saved to build his church.

When word spread of Joe's death and his unfulfilled dream, money began coming to the orphanage from all over the state to build Joe's church. Two years after his death, enough had come to start building. A year later, a little white church was completed. It had a porch and was named Little Joe's Presbyterian Church.

In 1955, an imposing new brick church was built on the children's home grounds alongside US-21. It has a high steeple, stained-glass windows, chimes, and a wide porch with massive white columns.

A couple of hundred feet away in a small, shaded cemetery is a flat concrete marker over the grave of Joe Gilland. It's behind the church. The porch can't be seen from there.

Love Valley

Home of the Man With the World's Strongest Teeth

In 1970, Joe Ponder, a long-distance truck driver, broke his neck in a traffic accident. He spent a lot of time in traction recuperating. One day while lying in bed looking at a rafter above him, he wondered if he could throw a sheet across the rafter and pull himself up with his teeth. He tried it and found that he could.

Joe began amusing himself by hanging from the rafter by his teeth. After he recovered, he went looking for other things he could do with his teeth. He started pulling a pickup truck with his teeth, moved up to his tractor trailer, then graduated to a boxcar. He bent a steel bar with his teeth and next thing anybody knew, he was flying around dangling beneath a helicopter, hanging on by the skin of this teeth.

As Joe's fame spread, he was invited to Circleville, Ohio, to lift the world's largest pumpkin, 343 pounds, with his teeth. He went on to Naked City, Indiana, where he lifted two naked women with his teeth. Later, Joe lifted a caged panther and a mule with his teeth.

Joe has also fired the world's fastest machine gun – 2,000 rounds a minute – with his teeth, and he had a special set of golf clubs made so he can play golf with his teeth. He can chip and putt okay, but has yet to hit an acceptable drive.

"Just can't get any lift on the ball," he says.

In 1978, while putting on a free show at his house, Joe attempted a "death slide" along a cable into his back yard swimming pool, hanging on by his teeth. His mouthpiece broke, and Joe fell 25 feet to the ground, breaking twenty-seven bones. Fortunately, his teeth weren't hurt.

Joe, who is available for paid performances, still puts on periodic free shows at his home, which adjoins the leather company he operates on Main Street. For information, call Joe at (704) 592-2010.

The East's Only Working Western Town

No motorized vehicles are allowed on Love Valley's Main Street, only horses. This street looks like a set for an old western movie. That's exactly how Andy Barker wanted it.

"This is a horse and cowboy town," he says. "Everybody in town wears western clothes."

Andy always liked horses, and while he was away fighting World War II, the idea came to him to build a western-style resort town when he got back home – if he did.

He did come back, went into the construction business with his father in Charlotte, prospered, and in 1954, he acquired a tract of land in the Brushy Mountains of northwestern Iredell County and began building his town.

Now incorporated, Love Valley has a mayor – Andy – and a town council. It's the only town in the East with a marshal, Ed McCoy. It has a hotel, a saloon, and a dance hall. The sidewalks are wood, and hitching posts and water troughs line the unpaved Main Street.

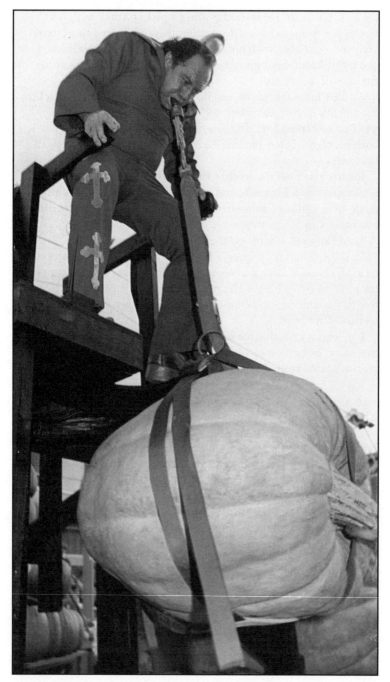

Joe Ponder lifts world's largest pumpkin with his teeth

Main Street, the East's only Western town

The town once had a jail, but it was closed by federal inspectors.

"Told me if I opened it back up, they'd lock me up – and not in my own jail," says the mayor, who has twice been a candidate for governor.

Numerous rodeos and other horse-related events are staged annually in Love Valley. "We have something every weekend during the summer," says Andy. There's no admission fee to the town or riding trails, and camping is available.

"This is not a tourist trap," says the mayor. "People are always asking, 'What's the gimmick?' They think there's got to be a gimmick, but there's not."

The Love Valley Road is 12 miles north of Interstate 40, off NC-115. For more information, write Andy at Box 265, Love Valley, 28677, or call (704) 592-7451.

Statesville

America's Oldest Hot Air Balloon Rally

Tracy Barnes, who in 1958 became the first person to fly a hot air balloon across the United States, designed and perfected several new safety features on the balloons he flew, and other balloonists began asking him to make balloons for them.

So in 1973, he settled in Iredell County, where rents were cheap, and began making balloons in an old chicken house.

The following year in October he held a rally to give the people for whom he was making balloons a chance to get together, get to know one another, and fly their balloons over the Iredell hills while the leaves were in their fall splendor.

Tracy called his company The Balloon Works, and it kept growing until it occupied four chicken houses and hit peak production of 300 balloons a year in 1979. Tracy sold the company in 1983, and it moved into a new plant in Statesville.

As the company grew, so did the annual get-together for customers. It evolved into the National Balloon Rally, one of the largest and most colorful spectacles of its kind. Once held in a pasture next to the chicken houses, the two-day event on the third weekend in October is now held at the Statesville Airport south of Interstate 40 off Amity Hill Road.

World's Second-Largest *Gone with the Wind* Collection

Bill Wooten was already a confirmed movie addict when as a teenager he went with his family to see *Gone with the Wind* when it came out in 1939.

He loved movies. He'd been going to movies alone since he was nine. He remembers having his mother write a note asking that he be excused from school because of pink eye, then spending the whole day in a theater watching *King Kong*.

But no movie before or since touched him like *Gone with the Wind*. It captivated him, enchanted him.

"It seemed to be the complete entertainment," he says. "Everything in it was perfection."

Bill is embarrassed to tell how many times he's seen the movie. Begin guessing around a hundred. When he wasn't watching the movie, chances are he was collecting items pertaining to it. His collection of newspaper and magazine clippings about the movie, still photos from it, posters and other advertising materials, books, sound track albums, and other items is second only to that owned by fellow collector Herb Bridges, a Georgian. Bill even has an original press book distributed before the movie came out. "So rare," he says, "that even David O. Selznick Studios doesn't have it."

Bill, a librarian and former radio announcer who began his collection while working in a Charlotte theater as a student at Davidson College, will show it by appointment. Call (704) 873-8835.

Lincoln

Lincolnton

George Fawcett's UFO Museum and Convention

George Fawcett was ten when he started a World War II scrapbook that grew to forty-eight volumes. It was while he was collecting material for his scrapbooks that he first came across a report of American pilots seeing strange objects in the sky over Germany. In 1947, when a pilot reported seeing unidentified flying objects over Mt. Rainier in Washington, thus sparking the UFO era, George was fascinated. He has remained passionately fascinated ever since.

A former YMCA director now in newspaper advertising, George has devoted much of his life to tracking down UFOs and proving their existence. He has collected and read more than 500 books on the subject and written one of his own. He has personally investigated thousands of reported sightings, gathered thousands more reports and documents, including previously classified reports of government investigations, and collected 800 photos of UFOs, plus models of UFOs and sculptures of alien creatures reported seen by witnesses he has interrogated.

The material overflows his house and garage at 602 Battleground Road. "It's godawful," he says. "It's all over the place."

For years, George has dreamed of establishing a UFO museum and study center to house his colleciton. But for now he makes do with exhibits in the UFO Room at his wife Shirley's Super Sub Sandwich Shop at 333 East Main Street.

George, who lectures widely on UFOs and even teaches a credit college course on the subject, also organizes a UFO convention held each June on Father's Day weekend at the Nature Science Center in Winston-Salem.

For information, write George at 602 Battleground Road, Lincolnton 28092, or call (704) 735-5725.

Mecklenburg

Charlotte

Tallest Building in North Carolina

The forty-two-story One First Union Building in downtown Charlotte is not only the tallest in North Carolina but the tallest between Philadelphia and Atlanta. Dedicated in September 1988, the building has a facade of rose granite and is of art deco revival design. It has been described as looking like an early, floor-model radio. Some 5,000 people work in the building, which contains a bank, offices, a shopping mall, and a YMCA. The building will reign as tallest for only a few years. Another bank, NCNB, is planning a sixty-story tower nearby, to be completed in 1992.

Wing Haven

When Elizabeth Clarkson married her husband, Edwin, and came to Charlotte in 1927 to see for the first time the house he had built for her, she found it sitting on an outlying red clay lot with a single spindly willow oak to shelter it.

This would not do, she said. So they bought some adjoining lots and set about building a garden. For years, on anniversaries, birthdays, and other special occasions, they gave each other 1,000 bricks. They used these bricks to build a walled 3 1/2-acre garden with stream, pools, walkways, trees, shrubs, and flowers that became not only a sanctuary for birds but also a place of respite for anybody seeking peace, quiet, and a touch of nature in the center of teeming Charlotte.

Birds flock to the garden with its many feeders, and 130 species have been spotted there, including green herons, kingfishers, and wood ducks. Many of the birds are so tame that they feed from Elizabeth's hand.

In 1975, the Clarksons gave their garden to a foundation to be kept in perpetuity. It is at 248 Ridgewood Avenue in southeast

Charlotte's Myers Park area and is open Monday-Wednesday, 3:00-5:00 P.M., at no charge. Pictures of birds likely to be seen in different seasons are posted and trees, shrubs, and plants are identified by markers. For information, call Ann McElwee at (704) 331-0664.

World's Ugliest Statue of Martin Luther King, Jr.

In the late seventies, a drive was started in Charlotte to raise $68,000 to erect a statue of slain civil rights leader Martin Luther King, Jr. When the money was raised, Selma Burke, a black sculptor born in North Carolina, living in New Hope, Pennsylvania, was commissioned to do the bronze statue.

When the statue was unveiled in April 1980, it stirred quite a controversy. The problem was, said critics, that it didn't look like King. The face was too lean. The nose, chin, and forehead weren't right. It was ugly, they said. Just didn't look like him.

The sculptor replied that she had tried to capture the spirit of King more than the likeness.

"I put down what I felt more than what I saw," she was quoted as saying.

That didn't mollify the critics who said they wished she'd felt like making it look enough like King to make him recognizable. Some even suggested sawing the head off and replacing it.

But nothing came of it, and the statue still stands in Marshall Park on East Third Street downtown.

The *Only In America* House

Harry Goldhurst grew up poor on New York's Lower East Side. In 1929, at age twenty-seven, he went to prison for four years for a stock swindle. Twenty-five years after he got out of prison, Harry Goldhurst was internationally famous, courted by rich and powerful people such as Eleanor Roosevelt, Adlai Stevenson, Hubert Humphrey, and John and Robert Kennedy, all of whom were his friends. But he no longer lived in New York and no longer was he Harry Goldhurst. He lived in Charlotte and he was known as Harry Golden.

Golden moved to Charlotte in 1939 as a reporter for the *Charlotte Observer*. Two years later, he left the paper to start his own small, bimonthly newspaper, the *Carolina Israelite*, a personal journal that offered its 30,000 mail subscribers a mix of humor, human interest

World's ugliest statue of Martin Luther King, Jr.

stories, and liberal politics. Golden used his paper to crusade for civil rights long before it became a popular issue.

In 1956, a collection of Golden's newspaper stories became a best-selling book: *Only in America*. After its publication, Golden was in regular demand as a guest on TV talk shows and lecturer on university campuses. He went on to publish twenty more books, including a biography of his good friend and fellow North Carolina transplant, Carl Sandburg.

Golden reluctantly closed the *Carolina Israelite* after a serious illness in 1968. He died on Oct. 2, 1981, at seventy-eight. His last years were spent in the house that also served as his office at 1701 East 8th Street. The house remains much as he left it, a repository of his books, papers, photographs, and mementoes. Anita Brown, Golden's friend of many years, keeps the house in order, but few visitors ever come to see it.

"I run into people and they say, 'I'd like to come by and see all the things,' but they never do," she told a *Charlotte Observer* reporter on the seventh anniversary of Golden's death. "Well, some do, but there aren't very many."

Montgomery

Black Ankle

Black Ankle Fort

Black Ankle, a community near the Randolph County line, once had quite a reputation as a rough and rowdy bootleg liquor center. In fact, that's how the community got its name. Bootleggers would build many fires to distract law officers from the fires of their stills, and it was said that they got black ankles from walking through all the ashes.

The community was so rough that Lester Singleton, who admits to making a little liquor himself once upon a time, used to joke that Black Ankle ought to have a fort.

So he built one.

It started as a simple stone house for his family on his twelve rocky acres. It grew into a fantasy land, built mostly from junk that Lester, a trash hauler, salvaged from dumps and other places. To the front of his house, Lester added a big public room with stone furnishings, an indoor pool filled with bream and catfish. This he

Lester Singleton and Black Ankle Fort

made into a recreation room and display area for the old things and oddities he has collected.

Outside, he built covered walkways, gardens, a waterfall, a mystery house where gravity is defied, a fun house filled with gags and his extensive bottle collection, a spook house, and carnival-like game booths. All of it he enclosed in a stockade of bamboo and birch. Out by the road he put a sign that says BLACK ANKLE FORT.

"We're going to be doin' something as long as we live, you know it?" he says. "And I'd just as soon be doin' something like this as anything. I love to fool around here."

Lester's fort is on State Road 1354. Turn at Asbury Church, just off US-220, about one mile south of the Randolph County line.

Moore

Cameron

Antique Town

Cameron once was known as the Dewberry Capital of the World, but disease ravaged the dewberry vineyards (none survive) and commerce failed to find the town. Because it did not grow and remained essentially unchanged since the turn of the century, the entire town was named a historical district in 1983. That designation helped Cameron to grow into a mecca for antiques collectors. Isabel Thomas opened the town's first antiques shop in her house, the Old Greenwood Inn, in 1978. Since then, eight of the town's buildings have been restored and opened as antiques shops or malls, with more than sixty dealers working in them. The town is on NC-24-27, just off US-1.

Parkwood

Millstone Ghost Town

Nobody knows what happened to Parkwood or its residents. What is known is that the town was founded in 1880 after Lewis Grimm discovered a large deposit of conglomerite, a blue granite impregnated with chips of hard white quartz that was used for making millstones. He founded a company on the site of the deposit and began making portable grist mills. The town of Parkwood grew around the company, and it came to have several hundred residents, a company store, and a two-story hotel.

Then early in the 1890s something happened. The company closed and the town was suddenly abandoned.

"No one knows why they left or where they went to," says Moore County historian Thurman Maness. "The workers just rode off and left their houses and everything behind."

Up until the 1920s, the town remained intact and drew lots of curiosity seekers. But vandals and nature took their course, and all the buildings eventually collapsed. The stone remains are now overgrown with trees. The town site, which isn't marked, is in a valley about 50 yards off NC-22, just south of the community of Parkwood, which took its name from the old town, slightly changing the spelling.

Pinehurst

The Country's Largest Croquet Center

Pinehurst, known worldwide for its golf courses, may soon be equally well known for its croquet courts.

In 1982, the Pinehurst Hotel and Country Club installed four regulation lawn courts for croquet – an ancient game played with mallets, balls, and wickets and favored by the rich – and hired a croquet professional, Peyton Ballenger, one of only two such persons in the United States.

"I think it's going to be one of the great centers of croquet in the nation," Jack Osborn, president of the U.S. Croquet Association, said of the facility.

No other club in America has as many croquet courts on the same site. Professional tournaments are being planned for the courts, which can be rented by the hour. For information, call (919) 295-6811. Other sanctioned croquet clubs in North Carolina are at nearby Southern Pines, Salisbury, Linville, and Aulander.

PGA World Golf Hall of Fame

Want to see the world's finest collection of golf tees, pencils, balls, and clubs? How about Dwight Eisenhower's personal golf cart?

Want to know the year-by-year hole-in-one records for golfers, amateur and professional? Want to know the story of golf from its crude beginnings in Scotland?

If so, the World Golf Hall of Fame is for you.

Pinehurst, which sports five world-class golf courses, with more than a dozen other courses within a few minutes drive, became one of the country's first and finest golfing centers, so when it was decided that golf should have a hall of fame to honor its best players, like baseball's in Cooperstown, New York, Pinehurst was a prime spot for it.

The World Golf Hall of Fame opened in a $2.5 million shrine in 1974, and all of golf's big names showed up for the dedication by President Gerald Ford. The Hall of Fame has seen some troubled financial times since, but continues to operate as a nonprofit organization.

On Gerald Ford Boulevard off Midland Road, the shrine and museum are open 9:00 A.M.-5:00 P.M. daily. Admission is charged for persons over sixteen. For information, call (919) 295-6651.

Southern Pines

Writer's Haven

James Boyd, born in Pennsylvania, returned from World War I to settle in a house his grandfather built in Southern Pines. A Princeton graduate who'd studied at Trinity College, Cambridge before the war, Boyd had been encouraged to write by English novelist John Galsworthy.

He published several short stories in the early twenties, and in 1925 his first and most famous novel, *Drums*, set during the American Revolution, appeared to great acclaim.

Before his death in 1944, Boyd published five more novels, bought the local newspaper, *The Pilot*, and transformed his grandfather's house into a Georgian mansion with some thirty rooms. While Boyd and his wife Katherine lived in the house, which they called Weymouth, they made it a haven for writers. Galsworthy visited there, as did F. Scott Fitzgerald, Thomas Wolfe, and editor Maxwell Perkins. Sherwood Anderson wrote short stories at the house and North Carolina playwright Paul Green worked there on a play.

At her death in 1974, Katherine Boyd left her home to Sandhills Community College. In 1979 the college sold it to a group called Friends of Weymouth for $700,000, to be turned into a center for the arts and humanities. Scores of North Carolina writers have since come to the house for short periods as writers in residence.

Exhibits and special events are frequently held at the center, which is open to visitors Monday-Friday, 10:00 A.M.-noon and 2:00-4:00 P.M. Weymouth is on Vermont Avenue. For information, call (919) 692-6261.

The Nation's Largest Stand of Virgin Pines

Weymouth Estate, owned by novelist James Boyd, includes about 150 acres of virgin longleaf pines, some believed to be as much as 400 years old, the largest such stand in the nation. State foresters have compared the trees in significance to California's redwoods.

The pines are now overseen by the state parks division as part of the adjoining Weymouth Woods Nature Preserve, some 400 acres given to the state in 1963 by Boyd's widow, Katherine. The preserve, at 400 N. Ft. Bragg Road, off US-1, offers a nature museum and hiking trails and is open daily at no charge. For information, call (919) 692-2167.

Orange

Chapel Hill

Largest Post Oak in the United States

The biggest post oak tree in the United States is on the campus of the University of North Carolina, northwest of Old West dormitory. It's 94 feet tall with a crown spread of 92 feet. The trunk has a circumference of nearly 13 feet.

America's Oldest State University

The University of North Carolina, the first state-supported university in the new nation, opened January 15, 1795, on a wooded hill named for a small chapel called New Hope. The first student, Hinton James of Wilmington, arrived February 12, and within two weeks, forty more students were enrolled. They were

Old East, American's oldest state university dorm

taught by a faculty of two and lived in Old East Dorm, the cornerstone for which was laid in 1793. The building still stands and is now a national historic landmark.

Largest Natural Botanical Garden in Southeast

The North Carolina Botanical Garden offers 330 acres of plants native to the state, making it the largest natural botanical garden in the Southeast. Walking tours, classes, and a reference library are available to visitors. Plants are sold. The garden, on Laurel Hill, off the US-15-501 Bypass, is open Monday-Friday, 8:00 A.M.-5:00 P.M.; Saturday, 10:00 A.M.-4:00 P.M.; and Sunday, 2:00-5:00 P.M.

World's First University Planetarium

John Motley Morehead, chemist, industrialist, and leading bene-factor of the University of North Carolina, became intrigued with a planetarium he visited while a diplomat in Sweden in the forties. He liked it so much that he bought it in 1948 and shipped it as a gift to the University of North Carolina at Chapel Hill, making it the first university-owned planetarium in the world.

Since its opening in 1949, millions of visitors have come to the 500-seat planetarium on East Franklin Street on the campus. Built in Germany in 1930, the planetarium is one of the world's largest, capable of simulating the appearance of the sky from any point on or near earth for 26,000 years in the past or future on its 68-foot dome. From 1960 to 1975, all U.S. astronauts came to the planetarium to learn celestial navigation.

Morehead Planetarium, which also offers art and science exhibits, has shows nightly at 8:00 P.M., Saturday shows at 11:00 A.M., 1:00 and 3:00 P.M., and Sunday shows at 2:00 and 3:00 P.M. Admission is charged. For information, call (919) 962-1236 or (919) 962-1248 for the taped information line.

Hillsborough

Hog Day

No hogs inhabit Hillsborough. They are forbidden by law. There aren't even many hogs in the surrounding countryside. Hogs rank behind tobacco, eggs, poultry, and beef cattle in the county's lineup of agricultural production. But in 1983, the town proclaimed an annual Hog Day celebration. Why?

Well, some folks in town decided they ought to have a festival but didn't know what kind. So they held a contest in the county schools to let students suggest what to celebrate. A high school sophomore, a hog farmer's daughter, suggested Hog Day and won.

The celebration is held the third weekend in June in the center of town.

Randolph

Asheboro

Oldest Mountains in North America

Some geologists believe the Uwharrie Mountains of Randolph, Stanly, Davidson, and Montgomery counties to be the oldest in North America and among the oldest in the world.

These mountains may date back 600 million years and are believed to have once reached 20,000 feet. Worn by time, most of the peaks are now only 800 to 1,000 feet high.

Within the range are Morrow Mountain State Park, the Uwharrie National Forest, four lakes along the Yadkin River – High Rock, Tuckertown, Badin, and Tillery – and the North Carolina Zoological Park and Gardens.

A 33-mile hiking trail, developed by the Boy Scouts, is maintained in the range. The northern terminus is on State Road 1142, six miles southwest of Asheboro, the southern terminus on NC-24-27, six miles east of Albemarle. A detailed guide and map of the trail by Nicholas Hancock can be bought in area stores.

World's Second Largest Natural Habitat Zoo and Most Unusual Zoo Structure

Upon completion, perhaps a decade into the next century, the North Carolina Zoological Park will be the second largest natural habitat zoo in the world. With sections representing six continents and the seas, the zoo will cover nearly 1,500 acres. Only the African section is now open, but the North American section is under construction and expected to open in 1993. The Asian and seas exhibits will follow.

The African section features a huge plains exhibit where elephants, rhinoceros, antelope, and other hooved creatures roam free, as well as a tropical aviary where visitors can mingle with exotic birds amidst lush foliage. The African pavilion has been described as the world's most unusual zoo structure. Featuring four geographic regions of Africa – the tropical forest, forest edge, swamp, and plains – it contains 53,500 square feet under a Teflon-coated fiberglass roof stretched from three canted masts, the tallest 90 feet high. It is the only building of its type in the world.

The zoo may also have the only exhibit where the animals run free but the spectators are caged. After the chimpanzees learned that they could dig up rocks and throw them at visitors, often with painfully accurate results, the spectators' area had to be caged to prevent injuries.

The zoo is just off NC-159, 8 miles south of Asheboro. Signs direct the way from all major highways. From April 1 to Oct. 15, the zoo is open weekdays, 9:00 A.M.-5:00 P.M., and on weekends and holidays, 10:00 A.M.-6:00 P.M. From Oct. 16 to March 31, it is open daily, 9:00 A.M.-5:00 P.M., Christmas included. The zoo offers two restaurants, snack bars, picnic areas, two gift shops, and trams to carry visitors to exhibits. Admission is charged.

Coleridge

Louis Cox's Thermometers and Country Store Museum

The thermometer was a gift, one of those old thermometers that used to be seen hanging outside country stores, bearing advertisments for cigarettes or soft drinks, snacks or snuff.

This one advertised R.C. Cola, and it set Louis Cox on a quest to collect other old thermometers. In the pursuit, he kept running into other items common to country stores – signs, fixtures, equipment, old products, and containers for products long since forgotten – and he bought these, too.

Finally, he had so much that he needed a place to put it all. So he built himself a replica of an old country store on State Road 2895, 3 miles southwest of Coleridge, and turned it into a museum. Still, it is able to accommodate only about a fourth of his extensive collection of old advertising thermometers. The museum may be seen by appointment. Call (919) 879-3668.

Level Cross

The Richard Petty Museum

Richard Petty is the most successful stock car racer of all time. He has won 200 major races, a record unlikely to be equaled.

Richard followed his father, Lee, into racing, and Richard's son, Kyle, now races too.

The family built a large racing complex next to Lee's big frame house, and there, behind a monstrous portrait of Richard, whose fans call him "the king," is the Richard Petty Museum, which opened in April 1988.

Visitors see a short film about Richard's life, after which they may browse for as long as they want among Richard's many trophies as well as among the hundreds of items made for him by fans. Among the other exhibits is the driving suit he was wearing when he won his two hundredth race at the Fireball 500 at Daytona Beach on July 4, 1984, with President Ronald Reagan in attendance. Souvenirs and autographed items are offered for sale.

The museum is open every day 9:00 A.M.-5:00 P.M., except Sundays and holidays. Signs show the way from US-220. Admission is charged.

Seagrove

Early American Pottery Center

Underlying the rolling hills of Randolph and Moore counties is a blue-veined clay that makes good pottery. It was discovered in the 1730s, and by the 1740s a community of potters had begun to grow in the area. It became a principal pottery center in the early days of the nation's history. And some of the same families making pottery in the area then – Cravens, Coles, Owens, Teagues – are still making it today.

Revived in this century, the area's pottery – particularly that made by the late Ben Owen at Jugtown – became world famous, shown in many of the world's largest museums, including a permanent display at the Smithsonian Institution.

Examples of the area's pottery from its earliest days to the present can be seen at the Seagrove Potters Museum on US-220 on the north side of Seagrove. Opened in 1980 in the old Seagrove depot, the museum features more than 2,000 pieces of area pottery from the collection of Walter and Dorothy Auman (Dorothy was a Cole), who moved the dilapitated depot from its original site to a spot next to their pottery. The museum also features pictures of old area potters as well as examples of their work. Maps to the workshops of some thirty area potters are available at the museum, which is open without charge Monday-Saturday, 10:00 A.M.-4:00 P.M.

In 1982, a pottery festival was started in Seagrove. Area potters display and sell their wares as well as give demonstrations. The festival is held the third Sunday of November at Seagrove School (behind the lumber plant, just off US-220). A limited edition auction is also held. Admission is charged. Plans call for using profits from the festival to build a second, larger pottery museum in Seagrove.

Richmond

Ellerbe

The World's Oldest Long-Playing Record and Other Marvels of Presley Rankin

As a boy growing up in Montgomery County, Presley Rankin loved to prowl the woods collecting arrowheads, rocks, and other unusual items. As a man, he continued his prowling and collecting, but on a much greater scale.

As an avid amateur archeologist and geologist and as a big-game hunter, he traveled the world collecting artifacts, specimens, and trophies. He also collected coins, stamps, crafts, art, antiques, and tools.

As his collection grew, so did his house – until it no longer could accommodate his collections. Finally, Dr. Rankin, the only physician in Ellerbe, announced that he would give his collections to the town if a place could be provided to display them. An addition was made to the town library, and the Presley Rankin Museum was opened in 1986.

Among the exhibits is the oldest long-playing record in existence, certified by the inventor, Dr. Peter Goldnack; mammoth tusks found in Richmond County; the 130-million-year-old foot of a phytosaur discovered in adjoining Montgomery County; a full turpentine mill; and artifacts from North State Orchard in Ellerbe, once the world's largest peach orchard.

The museum, one block west of US-220 in downtown Ellerbe, is open Tuesday-Friday, 10:00 A.M.-4:00 P.M., and Saturdays and Sundays, 2:00-5:00 P.M. Admission is charged.

Hamlet

America's Longest Straight Stretch of Railroad Tracks

The Seaboard System railroad tracks that begin in Hamlet and run southeast to Wilmington have no turns for 78.8 miles and are the longest straight stretch of railroad tracks in America. Only a 300-mile straight stretch of the Trans-Australian Railway is longer.

National Railroad Museum and Hall of Fame

Hamlet has been a railroad town for more than a hundred years. It's a hub from which the Seaboard System sends freight cars in many directions. At one time, when passenger trains were still common, forty-two a day stopped at Hamlet's picturesque railroad station, the only railroad station in the state honored with a state historic marker. Now only one passenger train, the New York-to-Florida Silver Star, stops, once a day heading south, once north. But if you want to board in Hamlet, you have to get your ticket somewhere else, because the ticket window closed in 1983.

A group of retired railroadmen are determined to keep the town's railroad station alive, though, and they've opened the National Railroad Museum and Hall of Fame, a big name for a small museum, in two rooms of the station. There they display memorabilia ranging from old conductors' uniforms to dating nails used to tell the railroad when track ties were put down. A replica of the Raleigh, the first steam engine in the state, may be seen, along with a photo of the Seaboard Limited, the first New York-to-Florida train. One room is a reproduction of an old telegrapher's office.

The free museum, in the center of town, is open Saturday and Sunday, 2:00-5:00 P.M., but old railroadmen can be found at the station telling stories almost any day.

Rockingham

Reidsville

The Country's Second-Largest Horseshoeing Contest

Farriers from more than twenty states pound and rasp in the annual competition of the North Carolina-Virginia Horseshoeing Association on the second weekend in November. Started in 1976, the contest is second in size only to the national championships, which are held in a different place every year.

Senior, intermediate, and novice farriers compete in making different types of shoes, as well as in shoeing different types of horses and mules. The event is held at Flat Rock Farm on NC-158, about 8 miles west of Reidsville.

North Carolina Wild Foods Weekend

Just what is poke salad anyway? Find out at the North Carolina Wild Foods Weekend, where you also can sample peppergrass, clover blossoms, dandelion greens, daisies, cattails, thistles, dock, burdock, and many other plants commonly called weeds.

Edeline Wood, a wild foods expert and protégée of the late Euell Gibbons, leads seminars and foraging expeditions to identify, gather, and prepare wild foods. A grand wild foods feast is the highlight of the weekend.

The event is held at the Betsy-Jeff Penn 4-H Center near Reidsville. Participation is limited on a first-come, first-served basis for a fee. Participants may choose from two plans, one providing seminars and meals, the other including lodging in rustic dormitory cottages. For information, call (919) 342-1235 or write to Sandra Moss, 814 Summit Avenue, Reidsville, NC 27320.

Rowan

Cleveland

Grave of Napoleon's General?

The marker on the brick mausoleum is simple: "In memory of
Peter Stewart Ney, a native of France and soldier of the French
Revolution under Napoleon Bonaparte who departed this life
Nov. 15th, 1846, aged 77 years."

Was Peter Ney in fact Napoleon's famed general Marshal Michel
Ney – called "Red Peter" by some – who supposedly was executed
by a firing squad in Paris after the Battle of Waterloo? Many people
came to believe so.

Peter Ney was a school teacher who drifted into central North
Carolina and moved frequently. He worshiped Napoleon and had
astonishing knowledge of the Napoleonic wars. In books about
the French Revolution that he borrowed from libraries, he
frequently penciled in corrections. He possessed all the physical
attributes of Marshal Ney, even battle scars, and was, like Marshal
Ney, an expert swordsman. Once while riding in a parade in
Columbia, SC, he was recognized as Marshal Ney by a Frenchman
then living in Charleston.

In his classroom when word came of Napoleon's death, Peter
Ney fainted and that night attempted suicide.

While Ney made no public claims to being the marshal, he
reportedly confided to friends that he was and even told them the
story of how he escaped the firing squad and made his way to
this country. Questioned on his death bed, he acknowledged that
he was indeed the famous general.

"The old guard is defeated," he is quoted as saying. "Now let me
die."

Ney is buried in the cemetery of the Third Creek Presbyterian
Church in the community of Cleveland, off US-70, in northwestern
Rowan County, where he taught.

Salisbury

Luther Sower's Medieval Armory And Chastity Belt Forge

Luther Sowers doesn't know what brought it on; he just knows that the interest was there even when he was growing up on a farm near Salisbury.

"I can remember taking tin off the chicken house and making Roman armor," he recalls.

In high school, he made armor for Latin Club presentations, and even after he went away to study sculpture for five years at the Tyler School of Art at Temple University in Philadelphia, his fascination continued. After he returned to North Carolina to teach art in public schools in Wilson, his interest in ancient military paraphernalia grew even greater. He began making swords, dirks and other weapons, uniforms and insignia.

In 1974, he quit teaching and returned to his family farm where he built a small studio and foundry and began making military reproductions. Items of armor and chain mail, a sort of metal fabric impenetrable by swords, are a specialty.

A few years ago, Luther gained national attention when he saw a letter in the Dear Abby column from a woman who had a very jealous husband and thought his anxieties might be relieved if she wore a chastity belt. Her problem was that she couldn't find one.

Luther wrote Abby offering to make an authentic chastity belt for the woman, and the letter appeared in her column. The results: lots of orders for military equipment but none for chastity belts. Just in case, Luther had done a thorough study of chastity belts and was prepared to make them, although he said he would try to talk any prospective buyers out of the idea.

"The things were extremely uncomfortable and very unsanitary, horribly unsanitary, very difficult to clean," he said. "Anybody coming back from a long trip and unlocking the merchandise would probably not want to have anything to do with it."

Luther's studio and exhibits of armor and weaponry are 4 miles west of Salisbury on US-70 and may be seen by appointment. Call (704) 633-4170.

Spencer

The Nation's Largest Transportation Museum

At the turn of the century, Southern Railway built the largest steam locomotive repair shop in the South at Spencer. It included a thirty-seven-stall roundhouse and a repair shop the size of four football fields. In 1983, the North Carolina Transportation Museum opened in the old facility. Called Spencer Shops State Historic Site, it is the largest such museum in the country and the largest of any type in North Carolina.

Visitors can see a slide-show history of the shops in a yellow refrigerated car before entering the warehouse museum, where they can examine exhibits ranging from Indian canoes to airplanes.

A handmade Conestoga wagon, old fire-fighting equipment, and many old cars and trucks are displayed. Railroad cars exhibited include Doris, the private car of North Carolina-born tycoon James Buchanan Duke.

Other exhibits range from a huge collection of highway signs to functioning diesel and gasoline engines and old railroad lanterns. The museum, on Salisbury Avenue (US-29-70), is open Monday-Saturday, 9:00 A.M.-5:00 P.M.; Sunday, 1:00-5:00 P.M. There is no charge. For information, call (704) 636-2899.

Stanly

New London

Cotton Patch Gold Mine

Glenn Nance grew up near Denton in Davidson County plowing rocky fields, working in sawmills, and dreaming of gold.

"I've thought about gold purty much since I was a little boy," he said. "I would read these gold stories, how some got rich, some got killed, some went broke. I'd take a pie pan and slip off down to the branch and try to find some gold. I had it in my mind that I'd cut off one day and find some."

It took a while but Glenn eventually did just that. He was in the grading business when a fellow said he'd like Glenn to help him determine if there was any gold on his old home place.

Glenn made one cut along a hillside on the fellow's land and turned up gold aplenty.

"I took out five pockets of gold," he remembers, "and one of 'em carried thirteen hundred and sixty-seven quartz rock with gold and over one pound of pure nugget gold, some of 'em weighing over an ounce apiece."

Two years later, Glenn bought 22 acres of the land and within a few years he'd given up his grading business, moved into a trailer on the land, and taken up mining. He dug three shafts, doing all the work himself, hauling out the ore in 15-gallon buckets.

Later, Glenn opened the mine to amateur panners, but he sold it in 1983 and died in 1987. The new owner, Royal Dean, a civil engineer and amateur geologist, allows panning of the mine's ore March-October for a fee. Go east on Gold Street and follow signs.

Surry

Mt. Airy

Grave of Original Siamese Twins

Although there were recorded births of joined twins before the nineteenth century, the first such twins to gain worldwide attention were born in the Southeast Asian land of Siam, now Thailand,thus giving the description Siamese twins to all such children.

The twin boys, joined at the chest by a band of cartilage and flesh, were born of Chinese peasant parents in May 1811. Their mother named then Chang and Eng and required them as young-sters to strenuously exercise their connecting band until they were able to stand side by side and live as normally as possible.

At fourteen, while working as peddlers in Bangkok, the twins met and befriended a Scottish trader, Robert Hunter. Four years later, Hunter teamed with an American ship captain, Abel Coffin, to bring the boys to the United States in the hope of exhibiting them for profit.

The boys arrived in Boston in August 1829 and were an immediate sensation. They went on to New York, then to London, drawing huge crowds. As their fame spread, they went to work for flamboyant showman Phineas Barnum and became his second-most popular attraction after Tom Thumb.

By the time they were in their mid-twenties, the twins were touring the country on their own. They had won American

citizenship and taken the family name Bunker, offered them by a
New York man named Fred Bunker in a chance encounter at the
naturalization office. In June 1837, they scheduled a show in
the North Carolina town of Wilkesboro in the green foothills of the
Blue Ridge Mountains.

Tired of traveling and exhibiting themselves, the twins became
entranced by Wilkesboro's countryside and decided to stay. They
opened a store which failed, and two years later, they bought 110
acres in the Trap Hill community, built a home, and became
farmers and wood cutters.

The twins had longed for marriage and families but that seemed
impossible before they met Sarah and Adelaide Yates, daughters
of a neighboring farmer. A scandal ensued when the twins
appeared in public with the sisters, and the four were ordered not
to see each other again. They continued to meet secretly, however,
and Chang and Eng, desperate to be married, went to the College
of Surgery in Philadelphia and requested an operation to separate
them.

The twins had already been examined by some of the world's
leading medical experts, who had decided that separation was too
risky. Doctors at Philadelphia didn't want to attempt the operation,
but the twins insisted. Meanwhile, Sarah and Adelaide learned of
their plans, rushed to Philadelphia, begged them not to go through
with it, and promised to marry them as they were.

The four returned to Wilkes County and on April 13, 1843,
in their local Baptist church, Chang was married to Adelaide, then
nineteen, and Eng to Sarah, then twenty. The twins were just a
month shy of their thirty-second birthday.

The four moved into the twins' house and both twins soon
fathered children. With their families burgeoning and quarreling,
the twins bought land in the White Plains section of adjoining
Surry County, near Mount Airy, and built each twin a house a mile
apart. Afterward, the twins spent three days in one house, then
three at the other, never varying their pattern. Chang eventually
fathered ten children, Eng twelve.

The twins got along remarkably well considering that they had
different personalities and interests. Chang drank; Eng was a
teetotaler. Eng liked to sit up playing poker with friends; Chang
would nod off. Chang was irritable, Eng even-tempered. A keen
sense of humor in both helped them accept their predicament.

Once when they got into a fight atop a hay wagon, Chang held
Eng down.

"If you don't let go, so help me, I'll throw you off this wagon,"

Eng threatened. Then both broke into laughter, realizing the absurdity of the statement.

The two families thrived until the Civil War, when hard times came. After the war, Chang and Eng, then well into their fifties, were again drawn into show business to try to make money. While touring Europe, they consulted the top medical authorities in England, Germany, and France about separation, but it was again ruled out.

On the way home, Chang suffered a stroke, leaving him partially paralyzed and deaf. Afterward, he began drinking heavily and his health deteriorated even more, alarming Eng, whose health remained good. To no avail, Eng pleaded for Chang to stop drinking.

In January 1874, Chang developed severe bronchitis and chest pains and was told by his doctor to stay in bed, but when time came for him to move to Eng's home for three days, he insisted on going. At Eng's home, Chang was unable to sleep, suffered chills, and wanted to sit up at night, much to Eng's discomfort. In the early morning hours of January 17, Eng insisted that they go to bed. Chang agreed, and a few hours later, Eng awoke to discover Chang's labored breathing had ceased. He called for help, and family members rushed to his side. A son told Eng that Chang was dead.

"Then I am going, too," Eng said and became hysterical, sweating and twisting, as if trying to shake free of his dead brother. While some family members tried to calm him, others rushed to fetch the doctor 3 miles away in Mt. Airy and to tell Chang's family of his death. Within an hour, Eng had slipped into a coma. After another hour, he died before the doctor arrived.

Two weeks after the twins' deaths, their families allowed a limited autopsy. It showed that a small artery passed through their connecting band, which would have made separating them difficult at the time. It also showed that Eng was obviously healthy and apparently died from fright.

The families wouldn't allow the twins to be separated in death, and they were buried in a large tin coffin in the Baptist church cemetery. Eng's wife, Sarah, who died in 1892, and Chang's wife, Adelaide, who died at age ninety-four in 1917, later joined them in the plot. The grave is at Old White Plains Baptist Church on old US-601, 2 miles west of Mt. Airy.

Sonker Festival

Nobody is sure how the term originated, but in Surry County sonker is a crusted, deep-dish pie, usually of fruit (although sweet potato is also a favorite), that is a local specialty.

Arguments sometimes break out over sonker recipes.

Each year on the second Saturday in September, the Surry County Historical Society sponsors a Sonker Festival at the Edwards-Franklin House, a restored 1799 house off NC-89, west of Mt. Airy. The festival offers country music and lots of sonker. At other times of the year, visitors can find sonker on the menu every day at the Lantern Restaurant in Dobson, the county seat, 7 miles south of Mt. Airy.

Union

Monroe

America's Largest Rabbit Club Shows

The Union Rabbit Breeders Club is the largest and fastest growing in the United States, with more than 200 members in North Carolina and South Carolina. Twice a year, it holds shows where hundreds of rabbits of most known breeds are displayed, including some of the finest of their breed.

Breeds include New Zealand White, Californian, Netherland Dwarf, Dutch, Rex, Belgian Hare, Flemish Giant, Satin, and Chinchilla, among many others.

"There's a shape and size of rabbit for everybody in the world," says club president Les Everett.

Club shows are open to the public at no charge. They are held the second Saturday in March and the last Saturday in September at Dickerson Center off Johnson Street. For information, call Les at (704) 283-5430.

Old Hickory Game

For nearly 200 years, North Carolinians and South Carolinians have argued over the birthplace of Andrew Jackson, "Old Hickory," as he was called, hero of the Battle of New Orleans, seventh president of the United States.

North Carolinians claim he was born near Waxhaw, just north of the South Carolina line. South Carolinians say it was at McCamie Park, just south of the North Carolina line.

To settle the issue, at least temporarily, residents of Union County, NC, and Lancaster County, SC, got together and staged an annual football game, played by the best players from each county's four high schools. The winning team claims bragging rights to Old Hickory's birthplace for the coming year.

The game, alternately played in Lancaster and Monroe, is played in late August and is always preceded by a big parade. Call (704) 289-1541 for information.

Wake

Cary

America's Oldest Gourd Festival

North Carolina, particularly its piedmont, is purported to be one of the world's finest areas for growing hard-shell gourds. Such gourds, grown in scores of varieties, have both decorative and practical uses, and almost every conceivable use for them can be seen at Cary's annual Gourd Festival on the third weekend of September.

Cary calls itself America's Gourd Capital. The first gourd club in America was formed in the town in 1939, and two years later it started the country's first gourd festival.

The event draws hundreds of gourd fanciers from many areas to display gourds and exchange gourds, seeds, and ideas. It's held at Jordan Hall at 1000 North Harrison Avenue. For information, call (919) 469-4061.

Fuquay-Varina

World's Only Gourd Museum

Marvin Johnson was a math teacher and high school coach for twenty years before he quit to return to his home, care for his aging parents, and take up tobacco farming. One day he discovered in the attic some old gourds his mother had hung up to dry years earlier and decided to plant some of the seeds.

"It just grew from that," he said.

What grew was one of the world's great gourd collections – gourds from all over the world. Marvin eventually grew more than 200 varieties and became one of the world's top gourd experts and leading fanciers. He has developed new gourds and rediscovered gourds thought to be extinct.

He has grown thousands of gourds every year – and given them all away.

"Lot of people ask me, 'Why don't you sell the gourds?'" he says. "Doggone, I'm not interested. I enjoy givin' people the gourds and wouldn't enjoy sellin' 'em."

Marvin sent gourds all over the world to acquaintances he made through the American Gourd Society. And inevitably gourds came back. Painted gourds, carved gourds, gourds hundreds of years old. Gourds made into toys, pipes, hats, dolls, animals, musical instruments.

By 1965, Marvin's home was so filled with gourds that he built a house for them in woods nearby and opened the world's only gourd museum. He put this sign on the wall: "There's an old legend that says if you give or receive a gourd . . . with it goes all the beauty of life in health, happiness and other good things."

Thousands of people have visited the museum since it opened, including once-famous fan dancer Sally Rand. The museum is always open at no charge. Near it is a nature trail, and Marvin has provided picnic tables and restrooms on a nearby lake for visitors. The museum is on NC-55 South.

Lizard Lick

Lizard Lick Lizard Races

The story is told that a fellow named Pulley, generally called Ol' Man Pulley, owned a government-sanctioned liquor (generally called likker) still in eastern Wake County in the last century. Ol' Man Pulley was the official taster as well as maker of the likker, and along about mid-afternoon he'd be a little unsteady on his feet and feel the need for a walk.

The still was surrounded by a rail fence, and Ol' Man Pulley would walk around it, keeping track by tapping the fence with his cane. Lizards favored the fence for sunning, and Ol' Man

Pulley would whack at them with his cane as he went.

"There goes Ol' Man Pulley with his lizard licker," people would say.

And that, supposedly, is how Lizard Lick, a community of some forty souls, got its name.

Lizard Lick always had trouble maintaining its identity, primarily because people kept stealing the community's highway sign. But never did it face a greater identity problem than it did in 1975, when the state opened a new US-64 bypass around the community. With the main highway no longer passing through the community and its road number changed to NC-97, Lizard Lick was all but invisible to passersby.

Charles Wood, a Lizard Lick garage owner, wasn't about to let his community be bypassed and forgotten. He mounted a successful campaign to get Lizard Lick on state highway maps and started an annual Lizard Lick Festival with lizard races to attract attention to the community.

The event drew so much attention that Charles Wood was elected honorary mayor. He even opened a town hall and Chamber of Commerce in a building at his garage where he sold Lizard Lick bumper stickers, T-shirts, and souvenirs.

Each year to promote the festival Charles came up with a new gimmick. One year it was a plan to build an amusement park called Three Flags Over Lizard Lick. Another year it was a mock Lizard Lick University offering honorary degrees. The festival, with Blue Grass music, square dancing, and other events, grew so large that the community had trouble accommodating all the people, and it was dropped for a couple of years.

But demand for the return of the lizard races, also known as the Lizard Lick Olympics, was so great that Charles revived them in 1983.

The races (bring your own lizard) are held in September. For information, call Charles at (919) 365-6648.

Raleigh

First State Art Museum

From the 1920s the North Carolina Art Society campaigned for North Carolina to become first to open a state art museum. In 1947, the legislature finally appropriated $1 million to begin an art collection.

The museum finally opened in 1956 in an old State Highway Department building near the capitol. In 1967, the legislature authorized a new building for the museum, but not until ten years later was ground broken. The modern new museum, delayed by bickering and construction problems, opened in April 1983. It provides a home for the state's 6,000-piece collection, valued at more than $50 million.

The North Carolina Museum of Art, at 2110 Blue Ridge Boulevard, off the Raleigh Beltline near the state fairgrounds, is open Monday-Saturday, 10:00 A.M.-5:00 P.M.; Sunday, 1:00-5:00 P.M. There is no charge. Call (919) 833-1935 for information.

Home of History's Most Significant Man

Professor Edwin Paget has lost track of the number of times he's been honored as History's Most Significant Man, but he keeps a close count of how many times he's run to the top of 14,110-foot Pikes Peak in Colorado – 985 times by the end of the summer of 1983.

A retired North Carolina State University speech professor, Paget has been running up the mountain several times a week every summer since 1950 to draw attention to one of his many theories.

The professor believes that people die far younger than necessary and that they should get stronger, not weaker, with age. He believes that people could live to be 130 or 140 if only they would regularly get enough oxygen to their brains. The way to do that, he says, is by running uphill. That's why he spends his summers running up Pikes Peak. He intends to prove his theory.

Professor Paget, who won't give his age except to say that he was born a few years one side or the other of the turn of the century, is a fountainhead of ideas and theories. He originated the Baby Olympics – athletic competitions for children aged six months to two years – to encourage babies to get enough exercise to keep a sufficient supply of oxygen flowing to their brains.

He also is the father of many inventions, including the perfect dining room table for dieters. It begins rising as soon as a diner sits at it, quickly taking the food out of reach.

Hailed as The Great Rejuvenator by a South American group and once named "The World's Greatest Brain" by the Society For Intellectual Stimulation, the professor lives in a humble abode for one so significant at 2733 Everett Drive, where he can be found running up and down his basement stairs 340 times a day getting oxygen to his brain and keeping in shape for his summertime treks up Pikes Peak.

Some Curiosities of the North Carolina Museum of History

America's First Female Parachutist

Georgia Broadwick, called "Tiny" because of her diminutive size, left her home in Henderson as a young woman to seek adventure. She found it in Los Angeles on June 20, 1913, when she became the first woman, and only the second person, to jump from an airplane with a parachute. Broadwick went on to a ten-year career of parachuting at air shows before returning to Henderson and a job in a tire factory. Her story will be told in an exhibit of North Carolina women's achievements when the North Carolina Museum of History moves into a new building across the street from its present location at 109 East Jones Street late in 1991 or early in 1992.

America's First $1 Gold Coin

North Carolina was the site of America's first gold rush early in the nineteenth century, and by 1830, fifty-six mines were operating in the state. That year, a German artisan named Christopher Bechtler, who made clocks, watches, jewelry, and unusual pistols, settled in Rutherford County and opened a mint to produce gold coins. Miners flocked to his mint, which turned out more than $3.6 million in $1, $2.50, and $5 coins between 1831 and 1857. Bechtler struck the first $1 gold coin in America. The world's largest display of Bechtler coins may be seen at the museum along with tools and other items owned by Bechtler. Other displays of Bechtler coins are at the Smithsonian Institution in Washington and the San Francisco Mint Museum.

America's Largest Flag Collection

The North Carolina Museum of History's collection of historical flags ranges from the Revolutionary War to the Bicentennial and is the largest in the country. Many flags in the collection are Civil War regimental and battle flags. The oldest flag was carried in the Battle of Guilford Courthouse in 1781.

World's First Machine Gun

Richard J. Gatling, born in Hertford County near Murfreesboro, the son of a planter, became a strong abolitionist and moved north to Connecticut, where he became wealthy as a result of his agricultural inventions, including a wheat planter and the steam-powered plow. In 1862, he patented an invention that changed the nature of warfare – the first successful rapid-fire machine gun, which was named for him. The gun had six barrels and could fire 200 rounds per minute. The first Gatling guns were made at a machine works in Cincinnati and were first employed in battle at the siege of Petersburg against Confederate troops, who were awed by their bloody effectiveness. The gun was used by the U.S. Army until 1911, eight years after Gatling's death. One of Gatling's guns, an 1890 model, may be seen at the museum.

Carbine Williams's Gun Shop

David Marshall Williams grew up on a farm in Cumberland County and as a young man drifted into the business of making moonshine liquor. After a deputy sheriff was killed during a gunfight at a raid on one of his stills, Williams was sent to prison for murder. While working in the prison machine shop, Williams, with the warden's approval, designed a gun that would revolutionize the manufacture of automatic weapons. That gun, called the carbine, was compact, lightweight, and easy to handle, and it became the favorite weapon of American troops during World War II, when 8,000,000 carbines were made. The carbine not only won Williams release from prison; it brought him wealth and fame. A movie was made about his life starring Jimmy Stewart, and for many years Williams lived flamboyantly. Eventually, he lost and squandered his wealth and returned to live in a sharecropper's house on the family farm near Godwin, where he spent his remaining years puttering in his tiny gun shop working on new weapons. After Williams's death in 1975, his gun shop was moved to Raleigh, where it is now displayed.

The North Carolina Museum of History is open Tuesday-Saturday, 9:00 A.M.-5:00 P.M., and Sunday, 1:00-6:00 P.M. There is no charge.

World's Most Prestigious Barbecue Cook-Off

North Carolina has no official state dish, but if it did, it surely would be barbecue. No other state can claim so many barbecue pits and barbecue restaurants, so many family and community barbecues, so many part-time and hobbyist barbecue cooks pulling mobile cookers behind pickup trucks. In North Carolina, as nowhere else, cooking barbecue has been refined to art.

That's what makes the North Carolina State Barbecue Championship such an important event. The cook-off is not the largest in the state by any means, but it is by far the most prestigious in all the land. Usually there will be no more than three dozen participants, but all of them had to win preliminary local cook-offs to qualify and that can be very tough in North Carolina. So it comes down to a competition of champions.

The cook-off, sponsored by the North Carolina Department of Agriculture and the North Carolina Pork Producers, is held the first weekend in June at the North Carolina State Fairgrounds on South Hillsborough Street. Participants are judged not only on their barbecue but on showmanship as well. Visitors are invited to watch the cooking, which begins on Friday night, as well as the judging, which takes place on Saturday morning, and to quiz the cooks all they want about techniques and sauce ingredients. Beginning at noon on Saturday, they may eat their fill of the world's best barbecue.

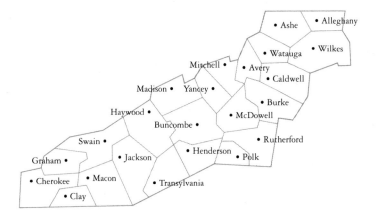

The Mountains

Ashe

West Jefferson

World-Famous Frescoes of Pregnant Virgin Mary

In the summer of 1972, a new Episcopal priest, Justin Faulton
Hodge, then forty-one, a native North Carolinian who had moved
away to New York to make his fortune, only to discover religion
at age thirty-six and enter a seminary, found himself assigned as
priest of two tiny mission churches in Ashe County.

One church, St. Mary's, at Beaver Creek on the edge of West
Jefferson, had thirteen members. The other, Holy Trinity, at Glendale Springs, south of Jefferson, was in such a state of disrepair
that it had closed.

Hodge was making slow progress in rebuilding the churches
until 1973, when, at a party in Blowing Rock, he met Ben Long, a
Statesville native and former Marine, who'd been studying the
ancient art of fresco-painting in wet plaster – in Florence, Italy.

Long wanted to paint a fresco for free in a North Carolina
church. He'd approached sixteen churches and all had turned him
down. Hodge accepted immediately, and the following year Long
did the first fresco, *Mary Great With Child,* at St. Mary's. After it
was finished, while he was working on two more frescoes at the
church, *John the Baptist* and *The Mystery of Faith*, Long was awarded
the prestigious Leonardo da Vinci International Art Award for
his work on the fresco of Mary and others in Italy, and little St.
Mary's Church suddenly found itself the center of international
attention.

In 1978, Long returned to Ashe County to teach a class in fresco
and create a huge new fresco of The Last Supper at the newly
restored Holy Trinity Church at Glendale Springs, before returning
to Europe to live and work.

In the fall of 1983, one of Long's students, Jeffery Mims of Southern Pines, created still another large fresco, of Jesus leaving his family. It is in the church's undercroft.

The frescoes revived the two churches, which now have more than 300 members. Hundreds of thousands of visitors from all over the world come to see them each year.

St. Mary's Church is off US-221 at old NC-194 at Beaver Creek near West Jefferson. Holy Trinity is on NC-16 at Glendale Springs. The churches are always open.

Second-Oldest River on Earth

Geologists say that only the Nile in Africa is an older river than the New, which is formed when its north and south forks, rising in Watauga County, join at the Ashe-Alleghany County line. The river — like the Nile, a rare north-flowing river — meanders back and forth across the Virginia line before flowing on into West Virginia, where it joins the Kanawha at Charleston.

Controversy arose over the New in the early seventies because of a power company's plans to dam it, but the project was stopped when the federal government designated a 26.5-mile stretch of the river in Ashe County as a National Scenic River.

Clear and swift-flowing, the river is popular with canoeists and rafters, and the state has provided five stop-off points along it for overnight trips. Several outfitters in the area rent canoes and give advice about the river.

Only Cheese Plant in the Carolinas

Mountainous Ashe County has long been a dairying center. Early in this century, several small cheese-making businesses grew in the county, but in the twenties the Kraft Company bought up the small companies and consolidated them in a plant in West Jefferson, where the company made cheddar cheese from 1930 to 1975. The plant was sold in 1975 to Doug Ruddersdorf and Jerry Glick, who expanded it and renamed it the Ashe County Cheese Company.

Cheddar, colby, and Monterey jack cheeses are now made at the plant, and visitors are invited to watch the process from a glassed viewing room Monday-Saturday, 8:30 A.M.-5:00 P.M. The company sells the cheese in an outlet across the street from the plant on Main Street. For information call (919) 246-2501.

Christmas Tree Festival

The first weekend in July may seem like an unusual time for a Christmas tree festival, but not if you're in the Christmas tree business. And Christmas trees are big business in the mountains of North Carolina, particularly in Ashe and Avery counties, where millions are grown every year.

Among the Christmas trees grown in Ashe County are balsam, white pine, and blue spruce, but the standard of the industry is the Frazer fir, which thrives only at elevations above 3,000 feet. The Frazer fir is said to stay greener longer and hold its needles better than any other Christmas tree. Twice Frazer firs from Ashe County have won the right to stand in the White House as National Christmas Tree in competitions among growers.

On the first weekend in July, growers in Ashe County gather for a trade show, and buyers come from all over the country to contract for delivery of trees in the fall. In 1987, West Jefferson started its Christmas Tree Festival to coincide with the trade show. Tours can be taken of tree farms, and tree-trimming and ornament-making contests are held. Decorations are sold and displayed by craftsmen and Christmas treats are sold. Call (919) 246-9550.

The South's Only Mountain Fen

Near the summit of 5,073-foot Bluff Mountain in southwestern Ashe County is to be found the only true fen in the southern Appalachians.

A fen is a swamp or bog fed by nutrient-rich ground water, not rain. This one is a botanist's dream, containing more than 140 species of plants, forty of them rare and endangered.

Among the plants to be seen are a pink-leaved, insect-devouring flower called the sundew, a gray lichen found no other place on earth, and Gray's lily, a rare, orangish-red flower named for Asa Gray, the Harvard natural history professor who first studied the wonders of Bluff Mountain in 1841.

In the 1940s, the mountain was bought by Mack Edwards, who protected it from developers and insisted before his death in 1978 that it always be preserved in its natural state. The mountain is now owned by the North Carolina Nature Conservancy, and visitors are allowed only on occasional guided tours in small groups so that the fragile plant life will not be damaged. Write the Nature Conservancy at Box 815, Chapel Hill, NC 27514.

Avery

Banner Elk

Woolly Worm Festival

Mountain folklore holds that the severity of a coming winter is predicted by the coat of the woolly worm, a black and brown caterpillar common in fall. If the woolly worm shows more black than brown, the winter will be bad.

Whether there is validity to this belief is frequently debated, and a long-term scientific woolly worm study undertaken by Dr. Sandra Glover at Appalachian State University in Boone has yet to reach any conclusions.

In 1977, Jim Morton, then editor of *Mountain Living Magazine*, decided he was willing to go along with the woolly worm theory, but the woolly worms he saw only confused him.

"They all looked different from each other," he says. "It was a matter of which was right and which was wrong."

It occurred to Jim that a simple way to determine which woolly worm was right about the winter would be to hold a race. The winning worm would be the official weather predicter.

Thus was born the Wolly Worm Festival. It is held each year on the third Saturday of October, and in past years it has been held on the practice football field beside the gymnasium at Lees-McRae College on NC-184 in Banner Elk (the location may change). More than 1,000 people attend the races, and as many as 350 have paid the $5 fee to enter a favorite worm.

The worms race on three-foot strings in heats of fifteen at a time. Winners then compete in crawl-offs until only one is left. The festival also includes mountain music and a gustatory treat called Woolly Worm in a blanket – a sausage dog made to resemble a woolly worm in a roll.

For more information, call Jim Morton at (704) 963-4228.

Where Marjorie Kinnan Rawlings Wrote *The Yearling*

Marjorie Kinnan Rawlings, a former newspaper woman, came to Banner Elk seeking coolness, peace, and quiet. She rented one of four cottages owned by Lees-McRae College and stayed several months working on her novel, *The Yearling*.

The story, set in Florida where Rawlings was living, is about a backwoods boy and a deer. The book became a best seller, won a Pulitzer Prize, and was made into a movie starring Gregory Peck.

While in Banner Elk, Rawlings got to know a young boy from the Grandfather Home for Children next to the college who came to help her with chores. The boy inspired her most famous short story, "Mother In Manville," about an orphanage child who imagined a family.

A retired Lees-McRae English professor who met Rawlings says that she kept mostly to herself in Banner Elk.

"No one knew her well," says the woman, who asks that her name not be used. "She was just another person around writing. We had many."

The four cottages on the campus were originally built for a music camp, and two of them later were torn down. The two that remain are used as residences by college maintenance workers. No one can remember which cottage Rawlings stayed in, and no markers have been erected to note her stay. The two remaining cottages are between the college gym and the children's home.

Beech Mountain

Highest Incorporated Town East of Rockies

Beech Mountain, a ski resort developed in the sixties, incorporated as a municipality in May 1981, causing the summer resort town of Highlands in Macon County to have to change its welcoming signs.

For years, Highlands, elevation 4,118 feet, had proclaimed itself the highest incorporated town east of the Rockies, but that honor was claimed by Beech Mountain, elevation 5,505.

Garbage Day

When Beech Mountain acquired its first garbage truck in 1982, it bought the biggest one it could find. The town has to haul its garbage to a landfill 25 miles away, and the town fathers didn't want the truck to have to make so many trips up and down the 5,505-foot mountain that the town sits atop.

So proud were the town fathers of their monstrous and expensive truck that they decided to hold a special ceremony to christen it with a bottle of champagne. Garbage Day was decreed. Hot dogs were roasted. Games were played. And the truck was properly christened. Everybody had a grand time, and when the first anniversary of the event rolled around and nothing was done to mark the occasion, some townspeople were upset. They thought the anniversary should be marked every year. Thus Garbage Day became an annual event held on the first Wednesday after July 4.

The day begins with a parade of garbage trucks from nearby communities, led, of course, by Beech Mountain's pride and joy. A hot dog roast follows. Townspeople dress themselves in trashy costumes, and the trashiest in three categories win prizes. The smelliest garbage truck is chosen. Admission is a bag of trash picked up on the town's streets or nearby highways.

One year, a group of middle-aged female residents arrived for the festivities in a big Buick convertible driven by a fellow in very flashy attire. The women were decked out in styles popular along Sunset Strip at midnight and smeared with enough makeup to make Tammy Bakker envious.

"They said they were the trashiest ladies in town," said Joe Archer, one of the organizers of Garbage Day, "and they wanted to know why somebody hadn't picked them up."

Linville

The Many Amazements and Wondrous Doings of Grandfather Mountain

In 1885, a young mining engineer from Wilmington, Hugh MacRae, went to work for the mica mines in Mitchell County and was so taken with the surrounding mountains that he prevailed upon his father to help him buy nearly 16,000 acres of land, including Grandfather Mountain, highest peak, at 5,964 feet, in the Blue Ridge Mountains. Four years later, MacRae founded a company and began developing the first mountain golf course and Linville resort.

In 1952, following MacRae's death, his company was dissolved and his holdings divided among family members. His grandson, Hugh MacRae Morton, came into possession of 4,100-acre Grandfather Mountain (so named because from one angle the mountaintop resembles the profile of an old man looking heavenward) and began developing it as one of the state's top tourist attractions.

World's Oldest Rocks

Geologists have found that Grandfather bares some of the oldest rocks to be seen on earth, more than a billion years old, and geologists come to the mountain to study what is called the Grandfather Mountain Window, which gives them a look at what the core of earth was like when time began. The oldest of these rocks, a granitelike gneiss, can be seen along Wilson Creek, which crosses US-221, on the south slope of the mountain.

Country's Highest Swinging Bridge

The mountaintop offers panoramic views, a visitor center with exhibits, and a natural wildlife area with bears, cougars, deer, and golden and bald eagles. Perhaps the biggest attraction is the Mile High Swinging Bridge, the nation's highest swinging bridge, which crosses a 100-foot deep chasm to Linville Peak. Built in 1952, the 210-foot-long bridge was designed by architect Charles Hartman, Jr. to withstand the weight of three million pounds and the high winds that regularly buffet the mountaintop.

Billy Joe's Tee

Near the bridge is Billy Joe's Tee, built for North Carolina amateur golfer Billy Joe Patton, who came within one shot of winning the Masters Tournament in 1954. Hugh Morton, a friend of Patton's, built the tee on the mountain's edge in honor of Billy Joe's near win so he could "knock a ball a mile." A golf ball won't sail that far off the 1,500-foot drop, but it will go a long way, and golfers who want to hit the longest ball of their lives are invited to do so. Both Ted Williams and Mickey Mantle have batted baseballs off the tee.

Eastern America's Highest Manned Weather Station

The visitor center also houses the highest manned weather station in eastern America. The mountain has some of the roughest winter weather in eastern America, and each day, regardless of conditions, Winston Church climbs the mountain to take readings. Winds of more than 100 miles per hour strike the mountain an average of twelve times a year. The highest wind recorded was 173 m.p.h. on April 8, 1988. Below zero temperatures are common in winter. The coldest was 32 below on January 21, 1985.

Masters of Hang Gliding

During summer and fall, a hang gliding team flies regularly off the peak to a landing in MacRae Meadows below. The tricky winds

Grandfather Mountain hang glider

around the mountain make it a spot for only the most experienced pilots. Each year in August, the top twenty-four hang glider pilots in the world are invited to the mountain to compete in the Masters of Hang Gliding Championship, a ten-day, one-on-one racing competition.

America's Finest Highland Games and Gathering of Clans

On the second weekend in July each year, thousands of people of Scottish ancestry gather on MacRae Meadows for the Grandfather Mountain Highland Games and Gathering of the Clans, founded in 1955 by Hugh Morton's late mother, Agnes. More than a hundred clans gather with tartans, kilts, and bagpipes for Scottish music, dancing, flag ceremonies, sheep dog demonstrations, and athletic competitions. The athletic events include caber tossing, highland wrestling, and clan tugs of war. Better Homes and Gardens has proclaimed this the finest Scottish gathering in America, and it is one of the 100 Top Events in North America.

Grandfather Mountain: Gathering of clans on Grandfather Mountain
Photo: Hugh Morton

America's Second-Toughest Marathon

A series of AAU-sanctioned track and field events is held in conjunction with the gathering, including the Mountain Marathon from Boone to Grandfather Mountain, the second-hardest marathon course in America (after the Pikes Peak Marathon in Colorado).

Grandfather Mountain: America's highest swinging bridge

Grandfather Mountain: Billy Joe Patton at his tee

Singing on the Mountain

Another popular event, at times attracting as many as 50,000
people, is the annual Singing on the Mountain held in MacRae
Meadows on the fourth Sunday each June. Founded by Joe Lee
Hartley, Sr. in 1924 as a family reunion, it was opened to all, and is
the only activity on Grandfather Mountain for which no admission
is charged. A day of gospel singing and preaching, the event has
attracted such celebrities as Johnny Cash, Roy Acuff, Bob Hope,
and Oral Roberts.

Grandfather Mountain is on US-221 east of Linville. For more
information, write Grandfather Mountain, Linville, NC 28646, or
call (704) 733-2013.

World's Most Complicated Bridge

The quarter-mile Linn Cove Viaduct around the base of Grandfather Mountain on the Blue Ridge Parkway is one of the world's
great engineering marvels.

The bridge, which has spiral curves going into circular curves
with curvature in two directions, has seven supporting tiers 150
feet apart. It was constructed with 153 50-ton segments, none
alike, only one straight. The $8-million bridge includes every kind
of alignment geometry used in highway construction and is the
only one of its type in America. It has attracted international
attention. Begun in 1979, it was completed in 1983 but wasn't put
into use until the final 7.7-mile section of the parkway was
completed in 1987.

World's most complicated bridge under construction
Photo: Hugh Morton

Buncombe

Asheville

Thomas Wolfe's House

Thomas Wolfe, North Carolina's most acclaimed writer, was born in 1900 in Asheville. For many years, his mother, Julia, operated a boardinghouse called Old Kentucky Home at 48 Spruce Street, where the family lived. The boarding house became the setting for Wolfe's first and most famous novel, *Look Homeward, Angel*, published in 1929. The autobiographical novel infuriated many people in Asheville.

Wolfe published only one more novel, a sequel, *Of Time and the River*, before his death from tuberculosis of the brain in 1938, but his editor, Maxwell Perkins, later gleaned two more books from his voluminous writings.

Wolfe, who was scorned by Asheville for many years, is now acclaimed in his hometown, where many things are named for him. The boardinghouse on Spruce Street is a state historic site, open to the public for a fee, May 1-October 31, 10:00 A.M.-12:30 P.M., 2:00-5:30 P.M. on weekdays, and 2:00-6:00 P.M. on Sunday. Each year on Wolfe's birthday, October 3, a celebration is held at the boardinghouse, featuring readings of his works and other events.

Graves of North Carolina's Most Famous Writers

Thomas Wolfe is buried, surrounded by his family, in Riverside Cemetery on Birch Street just north of Interstate 240 (take the Monford exit) near downtown Asheville.

His grave draws many visitors, who often leave flowers and other tokens of remembrance. His simple gravestone bears quotations from two of his works.

"The last voyage, the longest, the best," from *Look Homeward, Angel*, and "Death bent to touch his chosen son with mercy, love and pity, and put the seal of honor on him when he died," from *The Web and the Rock*.

Just down the hill from Wolfe's grave, a much smaller stone bears only the name William Sydney Porter and the dates 1862-1910. Porter was otherwise known as O. Henry, master of the short story.

Late in his life, Porter, a native of Guilford County, renewed acquaintance with his first sweetheart, Sarah Coleman, who had moved to Asheville. They married in 1907, and after Porter's death from alcoholism in New York, his wife brought him to Asheville to be buried. She and his daughter, Margaret, are buried beside him.

America's Largest and Finest House

George Vanderbilt was a well-educated young man who loved the finer things of life and had the money to buy them. Grandson of Commodore Cornelius Vanderbilt, builder of steamships and railroads, he had inherited a vast fortune and was using it to acquire a magnificent collection of art, books, and other fine things. But where to put it all?

Why not build the biggest and finest house in America just for that purpose?

So at age twenty-two, that's what he decided to do. He instructed a lawyer to begin buying the beautiful mountain land he had gazed upon so fondly while vacationing in Asheville, and within two years he owned 150,000 acres of it. He hired architect Richard Morris Hunt and landscape architect Frederick Law Olmsted to design and build his house for him.

It took five years to complete the 250-room mansion, and when it was finished, Christmas 1895, it was grand indeed. Vanderbilt married soon afterward and the house became home for him, his wife, Edith and their daughter, Cornelia. After Vanderbilt's death in 1914 at age forty-nine, his widow gave much of the land in the estate, where the nation's first tree farm and forestry school were established, to the federal government to form the nucleus of the first national forest, Pisgah.

The Biltmore Estate, still in the family, now has about 11,000 acres and operates a large dairy and winery. The grounds and formal gardens, including the largest azalea garden and finest English rose garden in America, are open to the public, as are eighteen rooms of the house, including the 72- by 42-foot dining hall, with its arched 75-foot ceiling, triple fireplaces, and the world's largest wrought-iron chandelier, and the library with its rich walnut wood and 20,000 leather-bound rare volumes.

Several movies, including Peter Seller's last film before his death, *Being There*, have been made at the house, which is open daily, 9:00 A.M.-5:00 P.M. for a fee. The estate is on US-25 South, near Interstate 40. For information, call (704) 255-1776.

Where Disney Doodled

In 1924, Thomas Cox hired an out-of-work artist who was visiting Asheville as a draftsman for his construction company. The artist went to work on the fourth floor of the Jackson Building downtown. The arrangement lasted only a few weeks before the young artist was fired for doodling. Walt Disney, then twenty-three, moved on to other work in California. Some of his doodles still decorate subdivision plats on file in the office of the Register of Deeds in the Buncombe County Courthouse.

F. Scott Fitzgerald's Room

F. Scott Fitzgerald, whose novels captured the Jazz Age of the twenties, was an alcoholic struggling to retain his talents when he first came to the North Carolina mountains to rest in 1935.

So taken was he with the area that in the spring of 1936, he moved his flamboyant wife, Zelda, from a Baltimore hospital, where she'd been making little progress from her mental illness, to Highland Hospital near Asheville. That summer he sold his home in Baltimore and moved into room 441 at the swank Grove Park Inn.

There he lived off and on for a year, drinking heavily (as much as thirty beers a day) and staying up late trying to write stories for magazines. Once he fired a shot in a suicide threat, prompting the hotel to require him to have a nurse.

Another time he showed up at Old Kentucky Home, the boardinghouse operated by the mother of Thomas Wolfe, Asheville's own famous literary son, pretending to want to rent a room.

"I don't rent to drunks," Tom's mother, Julia, told him.

By the summer of 1937, Fitzgerald was broke and depressed. In desperation, he went to Hollywood to become a screenwriter for MGM. He died there in 1940, a broken man, age forty-four. Zelda died eight years later in a fire at Highland Hospital.

The room where Fitzgerald stayed is still in use, but nothing marks it as special. The hotel has had many famous guests and considers Fitzgerald as no different from the others. The hotel is on Macon Avenue, near downtown.

Thomas Wolfe Memorial: Old Kentucky Home
Photo: Larry Tucker

America's Oldest Folk Festival

Bascom Lamar Lunsford learned to play the banjo as a boy growing up in the mountains. Later, when he became a nursery salesman, peddling apple trees to mountain homes, he would take along his banjo, sit and play, and ask his customers if they knew any tunes.

He collected hundreds of old mountain songs that way, and eventually he catalogued thousands, set more than 350 to memory, and recorded many for the Library of Congress and Columbia University. He even wrote a mountain song of his own that became a classic, "Old Mountain Dew."

Although he became a lawyer, he gave up law for his true love, mountain music and dance. He took mountain performers on tours around the country and throughout Europe, even to the White House. In 1928, he founded the Mountain Folk and Dance Festival in Asheville to perpetuate the music he loved. Later, he organized other such festivals, including the first National Folk Festival in St. Louis.

He appeared at his original festival every year until his death at ninety-one in 1973, although he had earlier turned over direction of the event to his son, Lamar. The festival, oldest of its type in the nation, has maintained the integrity Bascom set for it. No gimmicks. Just old-time mountain music and dancing.

"Go natural," he once said of his plan for the festival. "I won't caricature the mountain folks."

The festival is held the first week in August at Asheville's Civic Center on Haywood Street. For information, call (800) 257-1300; in North Carolina, call (800) 548-1300.

Black Mountain

World's Longest Golf Hole

The seventeenth hole at the Black Mountain Golf Club is 745 yards from tee to green, making it the longest golf hole in the world. It's par 6. The club, on Tomahawk Road, within sight of the beautiful Craggy Gardens of the Blue Ridge Parkway, is open to the public. For more information, call (704) 669-2710.

The Sourwood Festival

Sourwood trees are famous for one thing: the pale, wonderfully flavored-honey that is made from the nectar of their delicate white blossoms – the Cadillac of honeys, the beekeepers call it.

Perry Stone, a Black Mountain minister, liked sourwood honey well enough, but he loved the small, slow-growing sourwood tree, common in the mountains of North Carolina, for another reason – its beauty. "It blooms at a time when we need something, in midsummer," he says.

In the early sixties, Stone led a campaign to have the town of Black Mountain and its residents plant sourwood trees. His success caused Black Mountain to be called the Sourwood City.

So it was only natural that a festival would be organized to celebrate the tree. It is held the first weekend in August, when the sourwood is beginning to bloom. Sourwood honey is available year-round at the Chamber of Commerce. Call (704) 669-2300.

Enka

Nation's Champion Weeping Willow

The biggest weeping willow tree in the United States is in a cove
off Sardis Road, next to a spring on Charles and Linda Ford's dairy
farm. The willow is 97 feet high with an average limb spread
of 108 feet. Its trunk is 7.5 feet in diameter and nearly 24 feet in
circumference. Its age is estimated to be a hundred years.

Oteen

World Gee-Haw Whimmy Diddle Competition

Some call it a wooey stick, but to most it is a gee-haw whimmy
diddle, perhaps the oldest, simplest, and most fascinating of all
Appalachian folk toys. Its origins are uncertain, but it dates back at
least 200 years, and some believe that Indian medicine men used
the toy long before that.

A whimmy diddle is nothing more than a stick with notches cut
in one side and a propeller stuck on one end. Rub the notches with
another stick and the propeller turns. But there's a trick to it.

The edges of the notches must be rubbed with the finger or
thumb as well as with the stick. Rub the left side of the notches
with the index finger and the propeller turns right. Rub the right
side with the thumb and the propeller reverses. That's where gee
and haw, ancient instructions to mules and plow horses, come in.
Gee is right. Haw is left.

George Hardy, a retired Defense Department engineer who
helped build America's earliest missile-launching facilities, tested
whimmy diddles at Wright Patterson Air Force Base and found
what makes them work.

"We have to talk about directional damp," he says. "We're
converting vertical vibration to orbit through the use of directional
damp."

A lot of directional damp is employed on the third Saturday of
each May when the Southern Highland Handicraft Guild Folk Art
Center on the Blue Ridge Parkway, just north of Asheville, holds
its World Whimmy Diddle Contest.

Contestants compete to see who can make a whimmy diddle
gee and haw the most times in twelve seconds (sixteen is the
record). Awards are also presented for largest and most unusual

whimmy diddles, and many strange and elaborate, multipro-
pellered whimmy diddles are shown. For more information, call
(704) 298-7928.

George Hardy demonstrates four-pronged whimmy diddle

Swannanoa

America's Largest Southern Crab Apple Tree

The largest Southern crab apple tree in America is 200 feet north of the main gate of the North Carolina Department of Human Resources Juvenile Evaluation Center on old US-70. It is 35.5 feet tall with a crown spread of 48.5 feet. The trunk has a circumference of 6.5 feet.

Burke

Morganton

Home of America's Most Famous Living Witch

Joann Denton, former Sunday school teacher and go-go dancer, first gained national attention in 1976 at age forty-one, when she was charged under an obscure witchcraft law for accurately predicting a woman's death.

Joann, a diminutive woman who proudly proclaimed her breast size – thirty-eight – on her car license plate, admitted being a witch, but only a good witch, practicing "white magic." The charge was eventually dropped, but not before she had appeared on national television and was written about in *Time*.

Since then, Joann, who says she first realized she had psychic powers as a small child, has gained more attention by wrongly predicting her mother's death, by staging her own mock funeral, by performing psychic feats at a séance for an *Esquire* writer, by running for mayor of Morganton, and by opening her home, Gray Shadows, as a church.

The house, an ivy-covered stone cottage at 208 Lenoir Road (NC-18 north), just three blocks on the same street from the home of former Senator Sam Ervin of Watergate fame, is decorated with such items as a skull and a coffin.

Gray Shadows, home of most famous witch

H. Allen Smith's Totem Pole and Ashes

H. Allen Smith, one of America's most popular humorists, author of more than forty books, died on a trip to California in 1976, during which he was to have appeared on Johnny Carson's "Tonight Show." His body was cremated and his ashes shipped by UPS to his home in Alpine, Texas.

Smith had requested no service at his death, so his wife, Nelle, and daughter, Nancy Van Noppen, buried his ashes in the back yard next to an Alaskan totem pole his publishers had given him many years earlier to mark the success of his third book, *Low Man on a Totem Pole.*

His wife dumped a cup of spaghetti and a glass of wine, one of Smith's favorite meals, into the grave, and tossed in a crumpled page from his notebook, which he never went anywhere without.

A short time later, Smith's wife moved to southern Florida, and his daughter had her father's totem pole shipped to her home in Morganton, North Carolina. Three years later, she got to thinking about her father's ashes off in Texas all alone and had them dug up and mailed to her.

For months the small package bearing the ashes sat on her kitchen counter. "I knew that was where my father would love to be sitting," she told her son, Allen, who frequently played with the package without realizing it contained his grandfather and later wrote a story about it all for the *Greensboro Daily News.* "He loved to be in the kitchen."

But in the summer of 1981, the family reburied Smith's ashes in the back yard of the Van Noppen home at 310 Shore Drive, where they are once again guarded by his totem pole.

Site of Frankie Silver's Hanging

Frankie Silver was a jealous woman, and one night near Christmas of 1832, suspicious that her handsome husband, Charlie, had been seeing another woman, she attacked him with an ax while he slept with their two-year-old daughter in his arms in their cabin in a cove along the Toe River.

She chopped his body into small pieces and burned them in the fireplace, then told Charlie's family that he had run off with another woman.

But Charlie's father was suspicious, and after a futile search for his son, he consulted a soothsayer in Tennessee who told him Charlie had been murdered. A search of the cabin turned up bones and greasy ashes in the fireplace. More bones and ashes were found in a hole near the spring. A smudge of blood was found on the cabin door, along with a big circle of blood beneath the floor boards. An old hound sniffed out Charlie's heart buried under the front step.

Frankie was charged with murder and taken to jail in Morganton. She never confessed, but while in jail she wrote a long, mournful song about the episode that was taken as an admission of her guilt.

On June 12, 1833, Frankie was hanged from a gallows on Damon's Hill in east Morganton, becoming the first woman executed in North Carolina. Copies of her song, "Frankie Silver's Ballad," were sold to the throngs that came to see her hanging. The song, fifteen verses long, has endured in the mountains. A later version, which changed Charlie's name to Johnny, became nationally popular more than a hundred years after Frankie's death.

The site of the hanging, the hightest spot in town, is at the corner of Valdese Avenue and White Street, now occupied by a private home.

Valdese

America's Largest Waldensian Settlement

Waldensians date back to the twelfth century in Italy, where the Protestant group frequently was persecuted by the Catholic Church until it won political and religious freedom in 1848.

A population explosion prompted Waldensians in the Cottian Alps to send a search party to the United States to look for a new place to settle. The party decided on a mountainous 10,000-acre tract in Burke County, and the first twenty-nine settlers arrived in May 1893. They were soon followed by others.

The plan was to form a commune and to pay for the land by operating a sawmill, but they had no experience at all and the plan failed. Waldensians were traditionally farmers, winemakers, and stonemasons, and the land was divided and sold to individuals who paid for it by following their own pursuits.

The group, which merged with the Presbyterian Church soon after arrival in this country, founded the town of Valdese, and a hosiery mill and commercial Waldensian bakery provided the industry to make the town successful.

Waldensians are now merged with the rest of the population, and their vineyards are gone. But many of the beautiful stone buildings built by the early Waldensians can still be seen, and in the 1950s, the Waldensian Presbyterian Church opened a small museum to keep the Waldensian heritage alive. The museum has since grown into a building of its own across from the church on Rodoret Street. There may be seen furniture, clothing, farm implements, and other items used by the original Waldensian settlers. The museum is open Sunday, 3:00-5:00 P.M., at other times by appointment. Call the church at (704) 874-2531.

Cherokee

Andrews

America's Longest-Lasting Wagon Train

In 1958, a group of people in Cherokee County decided that the state should build a road up Tellico Mountain to connect with a Tennessee highway leading to Tellico Plains. To draw attention to their plan, the group organized a wagon train to follow the proposed route of the road along Davis Creek, through Hanging Dog, and on up the mountain.

The state paid little attention, so the wagon train was organized again the following year, and the year after that, and every year since.

It has grown bigger every year. In recent years, it has included as many as a hundred covered wagons drawn by teams of mules, horses, and occasionally oxen, plus as many as 500 horseback riders.

The wagon train, carrying its own Porta-johns (don't you bet the pioneers wished they could've had such luxury?), now lasts for a week to ten days and follows back mountain roads and trails to different towns each year. It always culminates in a big parade through some mountain town on July 4.

Did the road ever get built, you ask?

"We never got it," says Don Ramsey, who has been on every wagon train from the beginning. "But we're still tryin'. We're still a-workin' on it."

For more information, call Don at (704) 873-2892, or write North Carolina Wagon Train, Inc., Andrews, NC 28901.

Suit

World's Biggest Ten Commandments, Cross, Testament, and Altar

At the turn of this century, a Bible Tract Society member named Ambrose Jessup Tomlinson came from Indiana to pass out his tracts to the largely illiterate people of the mountains of western North Carolina.

He met a small group who wanted to form a new church to find the true way of Christ. Shortly before a meeting of the group to establish the church in 1903, Tomlinson trekked to a nearby mountaintop to pray. There it was revealed to him what kind of church the new one should be.

Such were the beginnings of the Church of God of Prophecy, a church that now numbers more than 300,000 members in this country and eighty-five others.

Tomlinson, who became the first general overseer of the church, decided in 1940 that because Jacob in the Old Testament had marked the spot where he received his vision of a ladder leading from earth to Heaven, a primary mission of his church would be to mark sacred spots.

The first place he decided to mark was the spot where his own church was formed. The church bought more than 200 acres of land, including the mountain on which Tomlinson had gone to pray for guidance, and named it Fields of the Wood. There Tomlinson planned to create a holy place.

He proposed to begin by creating the world's largest Ten Commandments in concrete letters 5 feet tall and 4 feet wide on a mountainside across from where he had prayed. He died in 1943, before he could see his dream realized, but he did see the commandments spelled out on the mountainside in lime.

Since that time, the church has marked significant religious spots in Israel and the Bahamas (the site of Columbus's landing, spreading the Word to the New World), but the primary effort has been at Fields of the Wood.

The Ten Commandments have been completed in white-painted concrete. The world's biggest altar, a concrete structure 80 feet long, has been built on Prayer Mountain, where Tomlinson prayed. On top of Ten Commandments Mountain is the world's largest New Testament, an open concrete Bible 30 feet tall and 50 feet wide, with a staircase up the middle to a viewing platform on top that will hold fifty people. Nearby is the world's largest cross, a prone concrete structure 115 feet wide and 150 feet long, lined by the flags of the eighty-six nations in which the church can be found.

A replica of Christ's tomb may be seen, and an outdoor baptismal pool is used by thousands annually. To be built in the future are a motel and a replica of Noah's Ark that will double as a gift shop, according to the Rev. Ted Carroll, superintendent of the park.

Fields of the Wood is on NC-294, 18 miles west of Murphy, near the Tennessee line. It is open daily year round and no admission is charged. Picnic areas are available. For additional information, call (704) 494-7855.

Graham

Fontana Village

Tallest Dam in Eastern America

Construction of Fontana Dam, a Tennessee Valley Authority project, began on New Year's Day, 1942, as part of the industrial buildup for World War II. It became the highest dam in eastern America when it was completed in 1944.

The dam, which holds back the Little Tennessee River in a 10,000-acre lake 29 miles long, is 480 feet tall and nearly a half-mile wide. It is 375 feet thick at its base, and three million cubic feet of concrete were required to build it. Fontana Lake, which has become a popular resort and recreation area, has an average depth of 130 feet.

Haywood

Maggie Valley

World Clogging Center and Museum

"The word clogging, as far as we can trace it back, just started being used in 1935 in Chattanooga, Tennessee," says Kyle Edwards. "We always just called it mountain dancing up to that time. You see, here in these mountains you've got a mixture. You've got the Dutch, you've got the German, you've got the Irish, the Indian, the black. What it was was just a cluster of dances and they mingled together. It's the oldest dancing I know that's been created in the United States."

Kyle's family has been involved with mountain dancing for as long as anybody can remember. Back in the twenties, Sam Queen of Maggie Valley, who became known as the grandfather of clogging, formed a dance team and Kyle's mother, Elizabeth, and uncle, Kyle Campbell, danced on the team, which performed in the White House for President Franklin D. Roosevelt and the Queen of England.

Kyle and his wife, Mary Sue, danced on later teams formed by Sam Queen. Their son, Burton, became world champion clogger in

1981 at age eighteen. Their daughter, Becky, won two United States female clogging championships by age thirteen. The family organizes dance teams and tours the country with them.

In 1982, Kyle, a road grading contractor, built a huge barnlike building across from his house on US-19 in Maggie Valley. Called the Stomping Ground, the building has a huge dance floor and seating for 2,000 people. Kyle hopes to make it the world center for clogging. Dances and shows are staged nightly from April through November, and he is developing a clogging museum in one section of the building dedicated to his late mother. A fee is charged for shows and dances.

First Southern Ski Resort

Tom Alexander, a guest ranch owner, became the father of Southern skiing when he opened three ski slopes with rope tows on a hillside pasture at his Cataloochee Ranch in 1960.

Tom and his wife, Judy, had started their ranch in 1934 to take vacationers on horseback tours along mountain trails, and they had been looking for something to give them business year-round. Tom made several trips to New England to observe skiing and decided it might go in North Carolina. He built rope tows in his pasture and installed snow-making equipment to ensure that he had snow.

The slopes were an immediate success, and in 1968, Tom, who died in 1972, expanded his operation by moving a mile along the same ridge, where he cut seven new slopes starting at an altitude of 5,400 feet and dropping to 4,660 feet. On these slopes he built a double chair lift, T-bar lift, and rope tows.

Tom's success spawned other ski resorts. Ten now operate in North Carolina's mountains, attracting thousands of skiers each winter.

Cataloochee Ranch is on Fie Top Road, off US-19, 4 miles northwest of Maggie Valley. It's open for skiing daily, December 1–mid-March. For information, call (704) 926-0737 or (704) 926-1401.

Waynesville

America's Oldest Ramp Festival

Outside the Appalachian Mountains, a ramp is generally thought to be an access to a major highway, or a sloping passage connecting different levels of a building, or whatever. To mountain people, ramp means more. Good eating, for one thing. Bad breath, for another.

Ramps are small wild plants that grow in mountain woods. Members of the leek family, they resemble green onions and taste similar to garlic, only stronger, some say.

Mountain people eat ramps raw and cook them with eggs, potatoes, country ham, and other dishes, and many look forward to spring when the ramps make their brief appearance.

Back in the thirties, a group of old-timers in Waynesville took to going off to Black Camp Gap, between Maggie Valley and Cherokee, to hunt ramps each spring and cook then into favorite dishes. The group gradually grew as members invited more and more friends to go along. Soon, politicians discovered the group and the possibilities of attracting news media attention by eating the loudly flavored but little-known plants. The event became too unwieldy to hold in the woods and was moved into Waynesville, where it became one of the highlights of the year.

The event is now held the first Sunday in May at the American Legion Park on South Welch Street. American Legionnaires, who sponsor it, fan out through the mountains gathering twenty or so bushels of ramps to assure that everybody who wants to taste one has the opportunity.

Dinners of country ham and ramps, barbecued chicken and ramps are sold, and the entertainment includes mountain music and dancing. But the high spot of the day is the ramp-eating contest. Winners have been known to eat as many as ninety raw ramps, and only the people closest to them know how long it takes them to recover.

"The scent will stay with you," says American Legion Adjutant Willard Francis. "You can smell them on a person's breath for four or five days – and it smells terrible."

For more information, call Francis at (704) 456-8691.

Other ramp festivals are held at Barnardsville in Buncombe County and Cherokee in Swain County.

Henderson

Bat Cave

World's Largest Fissure Cave

Nobody knows for sure just how extensive Bat Cave is, for it has never been fully mapped, but it is believed to be the largest fissure cave in the world.

Most caves are caused by water seeping through limestone, but fissure caves are faults in the earth's stone innards.

The main room of Bat Cave is 85 feet high and more than 300 feet long. It once was the home of a great flock of bats, but most have been driven away or killed by marauding visitors who have also destroyed other delicate plant and animal life at the cave as well as marring its walls.

Privately owned, the cave is now protected by the North Carolina Nature Conservancy, which limits visitors to occasional guided tours. Write the conservancy at Box 815, Chapel Hill 27514.

Where *Ben Hur*, the Play, Was Written

Perhaps it was prescient of Colonel Thomas Turner that he chose a literary name for the new inn he opened in 1892. He named it Esmerelda, for a novel written by Frances Hogdson Burnett while she was staying nearby. Whatever his intentions, his inn soon attracted a literary clientele.

Lew Wallace, a decorated Union Army general, governor of the Territory of New Mexico, ambassador to Turkey, and author of one of the best-selling books of all time, *Ben Hur: A Tale of the Christ*, published in 1880, came to the inn to work on the script of the stage production of his book. He finished it in room 109, and the play went on to a successful run of 194 performances.

Later, early movie producers discovered Esmerelda and made it a center of production. The 1915 twenty-reel epic, *The Goddess*, starring Earl Williams and Annette Stewart, was filmed here, as was *The Battle Cry*. Among the early movie stars who stayed at Esmerelda were Douglas Fairbanks, Mary Pickford, Gloria Swanson, and William S. Hart; later, Clark Gable was also a guest.

The inn burned in 1917 but was rebuilt on the same foundation alongside the highway that is now US-64-74. Now known widely for its food, the inn is open April-November. Call (704) 625-9105.

Flat Rock

Carl Sandburg's Final Home

Carl Sandburg, beloved poet, biographer of Lincoln, lecturer, and singer of folk songs, was sixty-seven when he and his wife, Paula, came to Flat Rock from Michigan looking for a warmer climate and better pastures for their goats.

They bought 243 acres on Big and Little Glassy Mountains and a fifteen-room house built for the secretary of the treasury of the Confederacy, and here Sandburg spent his final years.

A late riser, Sandburg took two upstairs rooms on the west side of the house, away from the morning sun, for his bedroom and writing room. It was in this house that he finished his novel, *Remembrance Rock*, and wrote his autobiographical memoir "Always The Young Strangers." It was in this house, too, in his wife's downstairs bedroom that he died on July 22, 1967, at age eighty-nine.

After his death, his wife, who died in 1977, sold the farm, called Connemara, to the National Park Service to be opened to the public. Except for the removal of his basement library to make room for service areas, the house is exactly as it was when Sandburg died. Even the goats and cats in the barn are descendants of the original stock.

The house, on Little River Road, off US-25, is open daily, 9:00 A.M.-5:00 P.M. $1.00 for adults, children 17 and under, free. Call (704) 693-4178 for information.

Hendersonville

World's Largest Gravestone for World's Largest Twins

Until they were nine years old, Billy and Benny McCrary were much like any other identical twins. But at that age they simultaneously came down with an attack of measles so serious that they had to be hospitalized.

After that, their bodies began to burgeon. Each weighed more than 200 pounds at age ten. At one point they were gaining weight at the rate of 100 pounds a year. Doctors determined that they had pituitary gland problems set off by the measles, but nothing could stop them from gaining weight. In high school, they weighed 400 pounds each and were formidable guards on their school's championship football team.

Shortly after high school, each weighed nearly 500 pounds. Unable to find jobs, they helped their father on his farm near Hendersonville, getting around to their chores on minibikes.

They rode their minibikes in Hendersonville's Apple Festival parade one year and somebody saw them and asked them to appear at two motorcycle shops. On their second appearance, in Greensboro, photographer John Page took a shot of them from the rear on their minibikes that appeared in *Life* magazine and later in the *Guiness Book of World Records*, which proclaimed the brothers the world's largest twins.

From that point, the twins were in show business. They appeared in Las Vegas playing trumpets and telling jokes with a 400-pound go-go dancer. They became a wrestling team and worked up a daredevil routine on their minibikes. They traveled the world.

All the time they continued to grow. Both topped 800 pounds before diets brought them back to the 700-pound range, where they stayed.

Their size (Billy's waist was 84 inches, Benny's 81) caused them many problems. They drove separate, reinforced, and specially equipped cars. Each had to buy two seats in airliners and neither could get into an airliner toilet (Billy once became trapped in one and had to be cut out after an emergency landing). Their own

Benny McCrary at grave of brother Billy
World's largest gravestone for world's largest twins
Photo: Buddy Chapman

furniture had to be reinforced and they carried small jacks to put under motel beds to keep them from collapsing.

They often spoke of having operations to reduce their size, but the lure of show business proved too great and they continued in it year after year, putting off the operations. Then in the summer of 1979, Billy fell off his minibike in Niagara Falls and injured himself. Complications arose and he died on July 14, weighing more than 700 pounds. His body was returned to Henderson County and buried in the Crab Creek Cemetery, just off Kanuga Road, 8 miles west of Hendersonville.

His brother later erected what he says is the world's largest granite gravestone on the grave, leaving one side of it for himself. The monument, 13 feet wide, weighing three tons, features etchings of minibikes in addition to proclaiming the brothers the world's largest twins.

Original Angel from *Look Homeward, Angel*

The marble angel from which Thomas Wolfe drew inspiration for his first and most famous novel, *Look Homeward, Angel*, is in Oakdale Cemetery on US-64 west.

Carved by Italian sculptors, the angel stood for years in front of the Asheville monument shop of W.O. Wolfe, Thomas's father. Thomas thought his father was keeping the angel to mark his own grave, but his father sold it, and it now adorns the grave of Margaret Johnson, wife of the Rev. H.F. Johnson, president of Witworth Ferndle College in Brookhaven, Mississippi. Mrs. Johnson died in 1905.

Time has taken its toll of the angel. Both wings, a hand, and finger tip have been broken off but replaced and patched. The angel is now protected by a stone wall and high wrought-iron fence.

A bronze replica of the angel has been erected in Asheville's downtown Pack Square, not far from where the original angel stood outside W.O. Wolfe's shop.

Apple Festival

North Carolina is one of the nation's top apple-producing states, and 70 percent of its crop is grown in Henderson County. Credit William Mills for that. He was the first white settler in the area, and he planted the first apple orchard. Now 16,000 of the county's

Original angel from Look Homeward, Angel

primarily red and golden delicious and Rome beauties, and thirty-two packing houses ship them to spots all over the nation. Two plants make apple juice.

That gives Hendersonville all the reason it needs to hold a week-long apple festival every year, culminating in the King Apple Parade on Labor Day. The festival, held yearly since 1947, features an arts and crafts show, a quilt show, a gem and mineral show, beauty pageants, clogging and square dancing, mountain music, and contests for the best decorated apples, best apple recipes, and best apple window displays.

Jackson

Cashiers

America's Largest Fraser Fir

In the front yard of the High Hampton Inn, near the sixteenth hole of the golf course, stands the biggest Fraser fir tree in America. It is 87 feet tall with a crown spread of 52 feet. The trunk has a circumference of nearly 9 feet. Growing beside it, far out of its natural habitat, is a cypress tree.

Highest Cliff East of Rockies

Whiteside Mountain is so named because its southern face is a sheer rock precipice, 1,800 feet high, making it the highest cliff east of the Rockies. The mountain is in Pisgah National Forest, west of Cashiers off US-64 on State Road 1600.

A two-mile hiking trail beginning at a Forest Service parking lot leads to the top of the cliff. Markings on the mountain face are believed to have been made by the expedition of Spanish explorer Hernando De Soto in 1540.

Sylva

Mystery Rock

Jadaculla Rock is 42 feet in circumference, a soft, brownish green
stone covered with mysterious symbols, a puzzlement to
archaeologists, who believe the symbols were carved by Indians
perhaps 1,000 to 3,000 years ago.

The rock is named for a figure from Cherokee legend. Judaculla
was born of a virgin princess, fathered by the thunder. He used
mountain tops for stepping stones and fired lightning bolts from
his bow.

A 100-acre treeless field on the Jackson-Haywood county line
bears his name and was thought by Indians to be sacred. According
to legend, hunters once tried to enter this field, and Judaculla,
angered, leaped after them, stumbled, and caught himself on a big
rock.

After disposing of the hunters, he noticed his handprint in the
soft stone, then drew a diagonal line across the right corner of the
rock and informed all that death would be the penalty for any who
crossed the line.

The line and marks that resemble a handprint, along with many
other symbols, can be seen on the rock, which is in a one-acre
undeveloped park, the only park in the county with an Indian rock
carving as its only attraction.

The park is 9 miles south of Sylva on unpaved Caney Fork Road,
3 1/2 miles off NC-107.

Macon

Franklin

World's Rarest Rubies

Late in the last century, a farmer in the Cowee Valley near Franklin
found a big red stone on his land and took it to town to try to find
out what it was. It was a ruby, and it caused a sensation.

Tiffany & Co. in New York heard about it and sent a gemstone
expert to investigate. In 1893, Dr. George Frederick Knuz made
the first official report on the rubies, sapphires, and garnets of the
Cowee Valley.

Tiffany bought hundreds of acres in the area and dug deep shaft mines along Cowee Creek in 1895. After four years, the company gave up the operation because it was never able to find the source of the stones, which were spread along the creek and the surface of the ground.

Among those stones were pigeon-blood rubies, the rarest and most valuable of all rubies – found in only two places in the world: the Cowee Valley and the Mogock Valley of Burma.

Other commercial operations followed over the years, but all failed to find the source of the stones and folded. Still, stones were found by people who lived in the area, or who came to search for them along the creek. People who live in the area tell of finding rubies by the jarful as children and shooting them at birds in slingshots. The late Paul Shuler remembered selling a jarful of rubies for a dollar as a child.

So many outsiders kept coming to the valley looking for precious stones that in 1950, the Gibson family opened a mine to allow tourists to sift buckets of Cowee Creek gravel in search of them. The Holbrooks opened a mine the following year, followed by the Shulers the year after that.

By 1983, eighteen mines were operating in and near the valley, attracting thousands of tourists annually. Rubies and star sapphires weighing hundreds of carats have been found by lucky tourists at the mines.

Some mines salt the gravel with cheap, brightly colored foreign stones to mollify tourists who don't find valuable native stones. Others refuse to salt. Among them are Gibson, Holbrook, Shuler, Gregory, Caler Creek, Jacobs, Cherokee, and Sheffield. The Cowee Valley is about 6 miles from Franklin on Cowee Road, off NC-28. Most of the mines are open from April through October.

On the last weekend in July, a four-day Gemboree is held at the Macon County Community Building on US-441 South in Franklin. Gemstone dealers and collectors from all over America gather to show, sell, and barter their stones.

World's Largest Sapphire

Ernest Klatt, an Oklahoman who moved to Florida during the Depression and got rich selling real estate, came to Franklin to see the famous ruby mines in 1955.

So hooked did he become on collecting gemstones that he opened a gem shop in Ft. Lauderdale in 1958. Two years later, he moved it to Franklin, where he had bought other property. The shop, Ruby City Gems, grew to be the biggest gem and mineral store in the Southeast.

In the basement, Ernest opened a large museum to display the finest specimens of his collections. The exhibits include such rarities as petrified dinosaur bones, unidentified fossils, and red emeralds from a mine owned by Ernest. Also featured is a large display of fluorescents, rocks that glow in brilliant colors in the darkness.

Star of the museum is a 385-pound sapphire, thought to be the largest in the world, dug out of a North Carolina mountainside by a Cherokee Indian in 1970. The sapphire originally weighed 465 pounds, but an 80-pound chunk broke off while it was being loaded onto a truck.

Ruby City Gems is at 44 East Main St. Admission to the museum is free.

Highlands

Drive-Through Waterfall

Mill Creek falls 120 feet off Rich Mountain to create Bridal Veil Falls on US-64, 2 miles north of Highlands. The old highway ran under the waterfall and is still open to anybody who has an irrepressible desire to drive through a waterfall.

McDowell

Jonas Ridge

The Brown Mountain Lights

One of North Carolina's oldest and most famous mysteries is the origin of the reddish lights that sporadically glow over Brown Mountain on the Burke and Caldwell county lines. They've been seen since early in the nineteenth century. Legends have grown around them and songs have been sung about them, but nobody has ever been able to explain them, although many have tried.

The lights have been blamed on everything from UFOs to locomotives. Some attribute them to marsh gas, or foxfire. Others credit atomic radiation, electrical discharges, and light refraction from the atmosphere with causing them. Sometimes the lights are just a tinge to the sky, but at other times they seem to move, even to dance, dividing like cells.

They may be seen on clear nights only from a marked overlook on NC-181 at Jonas Ridge, or from Wiseman's View in McDowell County, just off NC-105, 4 miles from NC-183.

One legend holds that if a dating couple sees the lights, their love was meant to be.

Old Fort

Andrews Geyser

Andrews Geyser is not, alas, a true geyser. It is more accurately a fountain. Built in 1885 as a scenic attraction to mark the beginning of the long, twisting railroad climb across the mountains to Asheville, the geyser functions by gravity with water piped off a nearby mountain, spraying a constant plume about 60 feet high. It's on Mills Creek Road, off old US-70, northwest of Old Fort.

Mitchell

Altapass

Curviest Railroad Tracks in the East

The Clinchfield Railroad tracks from Marion to Erwin, Tennessee, top the Blue Ridge Mountains at McKinney's gap near Altapass. In the climb up the mountainside the tracks pass through eighteen tunnels in 14 miles.

In order to maintain a grade of less than 1 percent, 18 miles of tracks were used to traverse a distance of only about $3^1/2$ miles as the crow flies, as the expression goes in the mountains. At one point, the tracks loop 7 miles to ascend only 300 feet, and the loops end only 400 yards from where they began.

It took 4,000 men employing steam shovels, dynamite, mules, and oxen three years to build the tracks; 200 of them lost their lives on the job. When the tracks were opened in 1908, they were hailed as the most magnificent feat of railroad engineering in the East.

The Loops, as they are called, can be seen from an overlook on the Blue Ridge Parkway, about 2 miles north of NC-226. From this spot, it is possible to get fourteen different views of a train snaking up or down the mountain.

Lee Medford's Caboose Museum

As a young man growing up in North Cove along a famous stretch of railroad tracks called the Loops, Lee Medford felt himself drawn to the mighty steam engines.

His harmonica playing once got him a ride with a legendary engineer called Foggison Bill who could play music with his steam whistle. Later, Lee went to work on a railroad maintenance crew, then spent more than forty years salvaging wrecks for the Clinchfield, Carolina, and Ohio Railroad, which later became the Clinchfield, now the CSX.

After his retirement, Lee bought an old CC&O caboose and set it on a strip of track next to the pallet shop, across the road from the fire station, in Altapass, which once had been a railroad center. He refurbished the caboose and turned it into a museum telling the history of Altapass and the CC&O. He spends many hours there and is happy to tell stories of train wrecks to visitors and to play railroad songs for them on a hand-cranked Victrola.

Bakersville

World's Largest Natural Rhododendron Garden

Roan Mountain, which rises 6,285 feet on the North Carolina-Tennessee line, has more than 600 acres of rhododendron thickets, which turn the mountain pink with blossoms in June, creating a breathtaking natural spectacle of panoramic views from atop the mountain. No other area has such a spread of the common mountain shrubs.

The blossoms peak in mid-June, and on the second weekend in June, the nearby town of Bakersville celebrates the flowering with an annual Rhododendron Festival, featuring a craft show, square dancing, music, beauty pageants, and other activities. For more information, call North Carolina Rhododendron Festival, (704) 688-3113.

Roan Mountain is on NC-261, 13 miles north of Bakersville.

World's largest natural rhododendron garden on Roan Mountain

Penland

America's Oldest and Largest Crafts School

Lucy Morgan started the Penland School of Crafts in a single log building in 1923, primarily to teach spinning and weaving to mountain women. The school, first of its kind in the nation, is now America's largest, teaching hundreds of students from all over the world every year in such crafts as weaving, pottery, woodworking, metalworking, glassblowing, sculpture, jewelry, enameling, lapidary, even plastics.

Eight-week courses are offered in fall and spring, and shorter courses in summer. The school now has thirty-three buildings on 380 hilly acres, and its staff of seventy includes some of the world's finest craftsmen. Many of the faculty members have studios that may be visited, and exhibits of all types are regularly held. The school is northwest of Spruce Pine and can be reached from US-19-E or NC-226. For more information, call (704) 765-2359.

Spruce Pine

Minerals Museum

North Carolina is rich in gems and minerals. Rubies, sapphires, emeralds, even diamonds are found in the state. Minerals are found in forty-nine of the state's one hundred counties, and the state leads the nation in feldspar production. The state boasts of more than 300 varieties of gems and minerals.

The Museum of North Carolina Minerals has a study collection of more than 700 catalogued specimens. Exhibits tell about the minerals found in the state, and how they are mined and used commercially. The museum, on the Blue Ridge Parkway at NC-226, is open daily, May-November, 9:00 A.M.-5:00 P.M.; weekends in April. For information, call (704) 765-2761.

America's Most Famous Blacksmith Shop

Bea Hensley never knew why he wanted to be a blacksmith; he just always did.

"As far back as I knew how to eat, I knew I could blacksmith," he says. "I was just borned this way."

As a schoolboy, he was able to make whatever he wanted from metal, and he went on to work for an old mountain blacksmith named Daniel Boone before he opened his own shop.

By the time his son, Mike, was a toddler, Ben had him workng at the anvil, and father and son came to be a team of master blacksmiths, making beautiful music on the anvil as they worked, creating beautiful objects of metal.

"We do fifteenth- and sixteenth-century blacksmithing," says Mike, "beautiful blacksmithing but functional."

That includes andirons, chandeliers, gates, railings, and other elaborate decorative items. And the Hensleys do them so well that they have been called upon to do work for Billy Graham's home, for Richard Burton's and Elizabeth Taylor's Hollywood home when they were still together, for Colonial Williamsburg, and many other prominent places. Their work is permanently displayed at the Smithsonian Institution in Washington and has been taken on a tour of world capitals.

Foreign visitors come to this country with no other purpose than to seek out the Hensley's small basement shop on NC-226 near the Blue Ridge Parkway. Visitors from all over the country stop regularly at the shop to watch them work and hear them make the music of the anvil, something they do every year at the North Carolina State Fair.

"I do these things because it's a glory," says Bea, "and money don't enter into it. I like a vision and a challenge. A lot of people chase the rainbow to make money instead of doing what God wanted them to do and they miss the boat."

Polk

Lynn

House Where Sidney Lanier Died

Southern poet, musician, and critic Sidney Lanier, best known for his poem "The Marshes of Glynn," died September 7, 1881, at age thirty-nine in a brick cottage at Lynn.

Born in Macon, Georgia, Lanier had roots in North Carolina. His grandfather moved to Georgia from Rockingham County. As a young man, Lanier aspired to be a musician and taught himself to play the flute. He became a private in the Confederate Army and saw action in several battles before being captured while serving as a signal officer on a blockade runner out of Wilmington. While in federal prison in Maryland, he contracted tuberculosis, which eventually killed him.

After the war, Lanier walked home, and for the next two years taught school and wrote a war novel. He married and in desperation practied law for six years before moving to Baltimore, where he became flautist for the Peabody Symphony, published his first book of poetry and two books of criticism, and became a lecturer at Johns Hopkins University.

Ravaged by his disease, Lanier moved to a tent camp near Asheville in the spring of 1881, hoping to recover his health. In August, he, his wife Mary, and young son Rubin, rented a cottage in Lynn, where they hoped to spend the winter. Lanier died in the cottage sitting before its open bay window watching the sun rise over Howard's Gap. Shortly before his death, Lanier, proclaimed to be the last of the romantic poets, wrote his last poem for his wife:

So one in heart and thought, I trow,
That thou might'st press the strings and I might
draw the bow
And both would meet in music sweet,
Thou and I, I trow.

The house where he died, still a private residence, is on NC-108 and is marked with a historic marker in the yard.

Mill Spring

World's Largest Collection Of Running Edsels

Few other people liked it, but in 1958 when Ford brought out its new pucker-faced car, the Edsel, Willard Jolley loved it.

"When they came out, they were odd and see that's what killed 'em with a lot of people," Willard says. "But I liked 'em because they were odd. They were just odd enough to me to be pretty."

The Edsel, of course, turned out to be one of the biggest boondoggles in automotive history. Ford made only 110,000 of them and lost hundreds of millions of dollars before stopping production in 1960.

About a third of those cars still exist in one condition or another

World's largest collection of running Edsels

and Willard Jolley, a retired highway department worker, has more than forty of them, more in running condition than any other collector.

"I didn't mean when I started for it to come to anything like this," he said. "I was just wanting to get me a '58, a '59 and a '60, make me three nice cars, but I just kept a-buyin' 'em and a-buyin' 'em, and a-buyin' 'em, and I got in real deep here."

Willard displays his cars under sheds in a big field next to his house, about 100 yards off NC-108, about a mile west of Mill Spring, and he loves for people to come and look at them at no charge. He calls the place Edsel Acre, and it is marked by the tail fin of a large bomb. That's Willard's little joke. In automotive circles, the Edsel was called the E-Bomb. For information, call (704) 894-8357.

Saluda

The Nation's Steepest Railroad Tracks

The Norfolk and Southern Railroad connecting Asheville with Spartanburg, SC, was the first railroad into the Blue Ridge Mountains. Completed in 1886, it retains the steepest stretch of standard gauge tracks in the United States in its climb up Saluda Mountain from Tryon. In one stretch, the tracks climb 600 feet in three miles, a 4.8 grade. The tracks can be seen alongside US-176.

Tryon

World's Smallest Daily Newspaper

The Tryon Daily Bulletin, established in 1928, calls itself The World's Smallest Daily Newspaper. It is the size of a standard sheet of typing paper, less than a third the size of most newspapers. Published Monday through Friday, the paper has a circulation of about 3,000.

Rutherford

Bostic

Abraham Lincoln's Real Birthplace?

History books say that Abraham Lincoln was born February 12, 1809, near Hodgeville, Kentucky, but a lot of people in Rutherford County believe he was actually born in a log cabin on a steep hill above Puzzle Creek, off an unpaved road near Bostic.

Near the end of the eighteenth century, an unmarried woman named Lucy Hanks wandered from family to family in Rutherford County doing spinning. In the course of her travels, she acquired two daughters, Mandy and Nancy. Convinced that the children needed more stable upbringings, she placed them in the homes of others when they were ten or twelve. Nancy went to the home of Abraham Enloe, farmer, teacher, and community leader.

Shortly after the turn of the century, Enloe moved his family westward and established a farm on the Oconaluftee River (a reproduction of it can be seen at the entrance to the Great Smoky Mountains National Park near Cherokee). Nancy went with them, but unbeknownst to the family, she was pregnant. When her condition began to show, Enloe's wife became upset, thinking her husband the father.

Nancy disappeared from the household, and for months her whereabouts were unknown. She reappeared with a healthy baby boy and Enloe gave Tom Lincoln, an itinerant laborer, a team of horses, a wagon, and money to take Nancy to Kentucky and marry her.

Some Rutherford residents believe Nancy returned to the old Enloe cabin in their county to have her baby. After Lincoln became famous, many older county residents signed affidavits saying they'd seen Nancy there with her child.

Who was the child's father? Some believe it was Enloe; others think it was Richard Martin, who courted Nancy briefly in Rutherford.

This is the story told in a 1920 book, Abraham Lincoln, *A North Carolinian With Proof*, by Dr. J.C. Coggins, a Rutherford teacher and legislator.

Tom Melton, a Bostic insurance agent, farmer, and former principal of Bostic School, believes it is true. He has located the remains of the stone cellar of the old Enloe cabin above Puzzle Creek and frequently leads visitors through the woods and undergrowth to see them. He requires each visitor to carry a stone to place atop a pile he has created at the site as a marker. Some day he hopes to have the site preserved and a more suitable marker erected. For more information, call Tom at (704) 245-4731, or (704) 245-0853.

Chimney Rock

Ghost Riders in the Sky

There are different tales about how Chimney Rock got its name. A huge pillar of stone rising from the base of a steep cliff high on the side of Chimney Rock Mountain, the rock does resemble a smokestack, and some think that early settlers gave it the name after seeing morning mist rising from it. Others say the name came from Indians who used it to send smoke signals.

Whichever the case, the rock has always attracted attention and given birth to many legends. Indians thought that the area around the rock was inhabited by a ghost tribe of little people.

Many indeed are the ghost sightings reported at Chimney Rock. In 1811, newspapers carried reports of a ghostly cavalry battle in the sky over the rock, complete with sound, and verified by several witnesses from different locations.

The rock is now a commercial tourist attraction. Visitors may drive to an area near its base, then ride elevators in shafts blasted deep inside the mountain to a visitor center from which they may climb onto the rock for a spectacular view of Lake Lure and the Piedmont plateau. The entrance is on US-64-74.

Wash Tub Races

The requirements are simple. It must be a galvanized wash tub; it must have brakes and a steering apparatus; and it must roll without benefit of any power other than gravity.

But there is gravity aplenty on the steep and twisting road from the top of Chimney Rock to the meadows in Chimney Rock Park, and that's the course for the annual wash tub races in mid-August.

Usually, more than a dozen wash tub pilots compete for trophies in two-tub elimination heats.

These aren't the only races at Chimney Rock. A sports car hill climb is held the last weekend in April.

Forest City

Charlie Yelton's Bottle Houses

In was 1970. Charlie Yelton had retired after working fifty years as a mill hand, and he was looking for something to do. He'd broken his leg helping a son set up a house trailer, and while he was recovering he saw a feature on television about somebody out West who'd built a small house out of bottles.

That was it. From then on, he knew what he would do. He would build himself a house with bottles. He started searching in dumps, carrying a burlap sack, gathering castaway bottles. Gradually, they accumulated, bottles of every type, size, and color.

He'd never built a house before and didn't know how to go about it, but he laid a brick foundation and started building walls with clear quart bottles, setting the mortar between them by hand. He framed the windows with green 7-Up bottles and created a blue cross under the front eave with Milk of Magnesia bottles.

It took him more than four years and 11,987 bottles to complete the house, and when he finished he filled it with . . . what else? . . . furnishings made of bottles and more unusual bottles.

After the first house, he went on to build two more smaller ones,

Charlie Yelton and bottle houses

Charlie Yelton inside his bottle house

plus a bottle wishing well and a bottle flower garden.

Thousands of people have come to see the houses, which fill with diffused light by day and often by night.

"It's prettiest when the moon is full and there's no leaves on the trees," Charlie once told a reporter. "It lightens up in there just like daylight."

Charlie's bottle village is behind his house at 937 Cherry Mountain Street. He welcomes visitors. Call him at (704) 245-2094.

Swain

Cherokee

Tuffy Truesdell's Wrestling Bears

Tuffy Truesdell was for three years the world's middleweight wrestling champion, but he was dissatisfied.

"I wasn't making any money wrestling, even with the championship," he says. "So I decided I was going to get me a gimmick. I went down South and got me an alligator."

Tuffy went on the road wrestling a 9-foot alligator, more often than not getting the worst of it.

"They were always trying to bite you," he says of the several alligators he wrestled over the years.

They frequently succeeded. He was bitten all over his arms and hands, got a severe gash in his head, had a knee ripped out, even suffered damage to a more personal part of his anatomy.

"Ripped the tail lights right off me," Tuffy says. "Alligators, there's no intelligence. We was on equal terms."

After Tuffy married a Canadian woman, he settled in Canada and opened a roadside zoo and alligator farm. That was where he bought his first black bear, which he named Victor. He and Victor were great pals and they often wrestled for fun. Soon the lure of the road began to tug at Tuffy again.

"I sold the zoo and went on the road with the bear in '62," he recalls.

Tuffy had trained Victor well and landed him several appearances in TV shows and movies. They also toured the country wrestling. But the wear of the road began to get to Tuffy again, and in 1977 he settled in Cherokee and opened a bear-wrestling tent next to the trading post owned by his old wrestling friend Osley Bird Saunooke, former Cherokee chief and heavyweight wrestling champion of the world, on US-441 North.

Tuffy gradually added more bears until he had a couple dozen and built a series of pits in which to display them. All of the bears have names and many perform. Tuffy and his employees still climb into the pits to wrestle and play with favorite bears, and visitors, who pay a small fee, may purchase vegetables and marshmallows to feed the bears.

The original Victor died in 1978 of a heart attack on a trip to Portland, Maine, in a stationwagon with Tuffy, who gave him mouth-to-mouth resuscitation trying to save him.

"We couldn't even talk about it for a couple of years," Tuffy says of Victor's death. "It was like losing somebody in the family."

World's Largest Bingo Game

Bingo games in North Carolina are limited to churches and charitable organizations and tightly restricted. But the Cherokee Indian Reservation isn't bound by these laws, and in 1982, the tribal council transformed an unused sewing plant into a 4,500-seat bingo hall and opened the world's largest bingo game.

Games are held every other Saturday year-round, and players come by chartered bus from all over eastern America for the regular $300,000 jackpots. In July 1983, Cherokee Bingo held the first million dollar bingo game, with 4,500 people paying $500 each to play. For more information, call (704) 497-2770.

The Oldest and Roughest Sport in America

Long before the first European explorers and settlers set foot in North Carolina, the Cherokee Indians were playing stick ball. It was a ceremonial game, played as part of ancient fire festivals, and it was rough. "The Little War," the Cherokees called it.

It was a simple game. Two teams of lean young men gathered in the center of a field. At two ends of the field were goals made of young saplings. Each player carried a short stick with a cup on the end. A medicine man tossed up a small ball, about the size of a walnut.

After that, it was a free-for-all. The object was to get the ball through the other team's goal by whatever means. The only rules were that the ball had to be lifted from the ground with sticks, and the sticks couldn't be used as clubs. Anything else was allowed – kicking, tripping, flailing, wrestling, boxing, hair-pulling, scratching, biting.

The game continued until one team attained a set number of points. Old-timers tell of games lasting two days and of players being carried off the field with broken bones and bloodied faces.

The game was highly popular on the Cherokee Reservation early in this century. Each community on the reservation fielded a team and took fierce pride in it. Betting of livestock, firearms, and knives was common at games.

High school football has replaced stick ball for the Cherokees, but the old game is still played once each year during the Cherokee Fall Festival on the second weekend in October. The stick ball game usually is held on Saturday afternoon on the high school football field. For more information, call (704) 497-3028.

America's Most-visited National Park

The Great Smoky Mountains National Park, 514,093 acres of wilderness, lies astride the North Carolina-Tennessee line and contains some of the highest peaks in eastern America. It attracts more visitors than any other national park, most of whom drive through on US-441, the single highway through the park, connecting the popular resorts of Cherokee and Gatlinburg, Tennessee. In summer, traffic sometimes backs up for miles along the highway as tourists stop to gawk at black bears that frequently gather at the roadside to beg handouts.

Terminus of America's Most Beautiful Highway

If there is a more beautiful highway anywhere than the Blue Ridge Parkway, it would be hard to imagine. The 470-mile scenic highway runs from the Shenandoah Valley in Virginia to the Great Smoky Mountains National Park in North Carolina, following the crest of several mountain ranges at an average elevation of 3,000 feet.

Begun in 1936, the highway was not completed until 1987, when the 7.7-mile missing link around North Carolina's Grandfather Mountain was opened. The highway has no commercial traffic, no stop signs, no stop lights, and no billboards. It does have numerous overlooks, exhibits, visitor centers, museums, hiking trails, picnic areas, and camping sites. The highway, which runs for 250 miles in North Carolina, has its western terminus on US-441, just north of Cherokee.

Living Cherokee Village

When the first European settlers arrived in North Carolina, the Cherokee Indians, a large and powerful tribe, controlled western North Carolina and parts of Virginia, Tennessee, South Carolina, Georgia, and Alabama. A proud and civilized people, they lived in villages and farmed.

But as settlers moved steadily westward, many battles were fought and the Cherokee gradually lost their lands. Still, early in the last century, Cherokees controlled great areas and some had built prosperous plantations and owned black slaves.

In 1820, the Cherokees instituted a constitutional republic, modeled on the U.S. Constitution, and in 1821, a Cherokee named Sequoyah introduced a Cherokee alphabet and a Cherokee literature was begun.

In 1828, however, gold was discovered on Cherokee lands, and settlers began pressuring the government to force the Cherokees

1750 cabin in Living Cherokee Village

Making a dugout canoe in the Living Cherokee Village

off. In 1838, 7,000 federal troops rounded up 14,000 Cherokees and marched them to the Indian Territories of the West, now Oklahoma. More than 4,000 Cherokees died on the way, and the march became known as "The Trail of Tears."

But about 1,000 Cherokees managed to avoid the troops and hid out in the Great Smoky Mountains. They gradually emerged and eventually got back 56,000 acres of the more than 7 million they had lost. This land became the reservation of the Eastern Band of Cherokee Indians, which now numbers more than 8,000 members, nearly 6,000 of whom live on the reservation.

The Cherokee heritage is preserved at the Museum of the Cherokee Indian on US-441 North, which houses the largest and finest collection of Cherokee relics in eastern America along with the largest collection of writings by and about the Cherokees. Displays and a movie relate Cherokee history and legends.

Adjoining the museum is the Oconaluftee Indian Village, where visitors can see a reproduction of a Cherokee village with demonstrations of Cherokee life before the arrival of settlers.

Unto These Hills, an outdoor drama about the Cherokees, is presented nightly in summer at the nearby Mountainside Theater.

The museum is open Monday-Saturday, 9:00 A.M.-8:00 P.M., and Sunday, 9:00 A.M.-5:30 P.M., in summer months; daily, 9:00 A.M.-5:30 P.M., the rest of the year. Oconaluftee Village is open 9:00 A.M.-5:30 P.M., mid-May through October. For information, call (704) 497-3481.

Transylvania

Brevard

Count Dracula Day

Transylvania County was not named, so far as anybody can determine, for the eastern European area, now part of Romania, that was the setting for Bram Stoker's famous novel about the vampire, Count Dracula. The county was formed in 1861 and named by decree by the state legislature, presumably because the two Latin words that join to form the name ("trans" and "sylva" meaning "across a wood") were appropriate to the heavily forested, mountainous county.

But after an advertising agency in 1987 suggested that the

county downplay its name because it had scary connotations for tourists, such an uproar of protest arose that Transylvania Mania Day was organized on Halloween Day in downtown Brevard. The annual event includes a Count Dracula look-alike contest, a Count Cotillion, a Flight of the Vampire run, and other events. But no stake dinner.

Pisgah Forest

America's First National Forest and Forestry School

Gifford Pinchot, the nation's first trained forester, began the first scientific forest management in America in 1892 on lands owned by millionaire George Vanderbilt, who was building a mansion near Asheville. Pinchot was succeeded by German forest master, Carol A. Schenck, who started America's first school of forestry, the Biltmore Forest School, in an area called the Pink Beds in 1898.

In 1911, Congress authorized the purchase of lands in the area for Pisgah Forest, the first national forest, and after George Vanderbilt's death in 1915, his widow gave vast acreage to the government to become part of the forest.

The campus of the Biltmore Forest School has been reconstructed using seven of its original buildings and opened as an exhibit at a museum called the Cradle of Forestry in America. Exhibits of early forestry and a movie may be seen at the visitor center, open daily. The museum is on US-276, 5 miles south of the Blue Ridge Parkway. The forest offers many camping and recreational areas.

The Original Waterslide

Waterslides are fairly recent developments in the amusement business, but this waterslide has been in use probably for hundreds of years. Indians are believed to have been the first people to enjoy themselves sliding down Sliding Rock.

Looking Glass Creek spreads to a thin sheet as it courses 60 feet over the broad slick rock into a clear pool 8 feet deep.

The rock has been a popular recreation site for decades, and even Lassie, the famous movie dog, once slid down it for a scene in a television show.

The rock is smooth enough to slide on without a mat, but a double-layered swimsuit is advisable for tender rumps. The U.S.

Original waterslide
Photo: Clay Nolen

Forestry Service has built bathhouses and a parking area at the top of the falls, which is on US-276, 8 miles north of NC-280.

Sapphire

Highest Waterfall in Eastern America

The Whitewater River drops more than 411 feet in two levels over the side of Round Mountain to create Whitewater Falls, the highest waterfall in eastern America, more than 200 feet higher (but considerably narrower) than famed Niagara Falls. The waterfall is on an unpaved road 10 miles off US-64 near the South Carolina line. A sign on US-64 directs the way.

Watauga

Blowing Rock

Where Snow Falls Upwards

The resort town of Blowing Rock got its name from a peculiar rock outcropping that overlooks the Johns River Valley nearly 3,000 feet below.

Legend has it that the wind always blows at Blowing Rock, often coming on updrafts funneled from the rocky gorge below, and in winter storms, falling snow is sometimes caught in the currents and whipped upward instead of down. When the winds are blowing with sufficient force, light objects, such as handkerchiefs, tossed from the rock will be brought back to their owners.

Indian legend tells of a despondent brave, rejected by his maiden, who flung himself from the rock only to be caught by the currents and returned to his remorseful lover. The rock is a popular, privately owned tourist attraction and admission is charged.

South's First Theme Amusement Park

The East Tennessee and Western North Carolina Railroad, a narrow-gauge line between Boone and Johnson City, Tennessee, opened the northwestern mountains to development at the end

Highest waterfall in Eastern America
Photo: Clay Nolen

of the last century. The railroad's small steam engines ran over the longest narrow-gauge track in the country and became affectionately known as "Tweetsie" because of their shrill whistles. Floods that washed out the tracks in 1940 brought the railroad's end.

In 1957, Grover Robbins, a local businessman, bought the line's engine No. 12, built three miles of track for it on a hillside on US-221-321 between Blowing Rock and Boone, and opened it as the South's first theme amusement park.

Tweetsie Railroad is open daily from Memorial Day to Labor Day and weekends in September and October. Call (704) 264-9061 for information.

Tweetsie R.R., the South's first theme amusement park

Wilkes

Wilkeboro

Jail Where Tom Dooley Was Held

There are those who still maintain that Tom Dula didn't do it, that he gallantly went to the gallows to protect his onetime lover, Ann Foster Melton.

Tom and Ann grew up together along Reedy Branch in Happy Valley near the Wilkes-Caldwell county line and were lovers by the time Ann was fourteen. Tom went away to fight in the Civil War, and in his absence, Ann, a beautiful young woman, married James Melton.

But Tom, a handsome lad, did return, and he and Ann picked up their relationship where they had left off, although Ann remained with her husband. Meanwhile, Tom also started a relationship with Laura Foster, Ann's first cousin.

Several months after his return from the war, Laura disappeared and was found dead in a shallow grave on a ridge, stabbed through the heart. Tom fled to Tennessee after Laura's disappearance but was arrested and returned to the Wilkes County jail, where he was held until her body was found.

Many believed it was Ann who killed Laura after she discovered that Tom was planning to leave with her.

At his trial, Tom was defended by the flamboyant lawyer Zeb Vance, a popular former governor, and the trial was given front-page coverage by the *New York Herald*. Tom was convicted largely on circumstantial evidence and hanged before a crowd of 3,000 on May 1, 1868.

John Foster West, a mountain writer who thoroughly researched the story for a book, *The Ballad of Tom Dula*, found it to be more a sordid tale than a romantic one.

Tom, he says, was a mean, low-life sort, feared by many who knew him. He was suspected of killing a man in Wilmington during the war who discoverd him having an affair with his wife. West believes the motive for Laura's murder was syphilis. Tom, Laura, Ann, James and Pauline Foster, who lived with Ann and played a role in the case, all were infected with the deadly disease for which there was then no cure. West believes Laura was killed because she gave the disease to Tom, who then spread it to the others.

But the romantic version of the story prevails, largely because more than half a dozen ballads were written about the case. One of them, "The Legend of Tom Dooley," became an international hit for the Kingston Trio in 1959.

The Old Wilkes Jail, built in 1858, where Tom was held, is now a free museum, open Monday-Friday, 9:00 A.M.-5:00 P.M.; Saturday by appointment. The museum is at 203 North Bridge Street. For more information, call (919) 667-3712.

Ferguson

Edith Carter's Whippoorwill Academy Museum

Edith Ferguson Carter, an art teacher, has long been intrigued by the story of Tom Dula and Laura Foster, so much so that she collected many artifacts about them and did a series of forty-five paintings depicting their story.

Her paintings and memorabilia are exhibited in a small school, the Whippoorwill Academy, built in 1880, which Edith, whose father was the last student at the school, had moved to a lot beside her house. The first floor, furnished with antiques, has been restored as a school. The second floor houses the Tom Dula museum.

Exhibits include the original headstone from Dula's grave, a doorknob from his home, and a lock of Laura Foster's hair. The museum, which is on NC-268 east of Ferguson, is open only by appointment at no charge. Call (919) 973-3237.

Tom's grave is only a mile from the museum off Highway 268. Turn right at the Yadkin River Bridge, park where the pavement ends, and walk along the narrow dirt road that forks to the left.

Wilkesboro

Only College Library Named for Poet Laureate

James Larkin Pearson went through only six grades at the one-room Whippoorwill Academy near Ferguson, but he became one of the country's most acclaimed poets and North Carolina's first poet laureate.

As a young man, Pearson went to work as a printer for a political journal published in Moravian Falls called *The Yellow Jacket*, which had a national circulation of 300,000. He went on to become the paper's Washington correspondent, covering Teddy Roosevelt, before returning home to start a humorous paper of his own, *The Fool Killer*, which achieved a circulation of 50,000.

After turning to poetry, Pearson published more than 1,000 poems. The most famous, titled "Fifty Acres," appeared in the New York Times. He became North Carolina's first poet laureate in 1953.

Pearson loved printing and always thought of himself as a printer first, then a poet. Five of his seven books of poetry were printed on his own press.

That press may now be seen, along with Pearson's manuscripts and 4,000-volume private library, at the James Larkin Pearson Memorial Library at Wilkes Community College on Collegiate Drive off NC-268, the only college library named for a poet laureate. The library was dedicated to Pearson on his 102nd birthday on September 13, 1981. He died two weeks before the dedication.

Yancey

Burnsville

Lumberjack (and Jill) Day

Trees are big in Yancey County. Pisgah National Forest makes up 40 percent of the county's land area, and timbering is the major industry. Lumberjacks abound, and they look forward to the day each October when they can prove whose skills are best.

Competitions are numerous. They include log loading and stacking, felling trees in precise areas, chopping trees with double-edged axes, and sawing trees with bow saws, two-man crosscut saws, and chainsaws. Since lumberjacking is no longer a one-sex trade, lumberjills compete in some contests.

The day-long event is held on the third Saturday in October each year at East Yancey Middle School, two miles east of Burnsville on US-19-E. For more information, call (704) 682-2420.

Mt. Mitchell

Highest Point in Eastern America

The peak of Mt. Mitchell, 6,684 feet above sea level, is the highest in eastern America. Once called Black Dome, the mountain was first measured by Dr. Elisha Mitchell, a University of North Carolina professor, in 1835.

After his measurements were challenged in 1855 by Congressman Thomas Clingman, Mitchell returned to the mountain in 1857 to verify his findings and fell to his death over a 40-foot waterfall. He is buried on the summit of the mountain, which was named for him after his death.

In 1915, the state bought 1,224 acres of Mt. Mitchell and made it North Carolina's first state park. The summit can be reached on NC-128 off the Blue Ridge Parkway. A tower at the top provides a beautiful panoramic view.

Index

About the Author

Jerry Bledsoe is a columnist for the *Greensboro News & Record*. His columns have delighted readers for many years and won him five national honors, including two Ernie Pyle Awards. He has been a columnist for the *Charlotte Observer*, and has served as a contributing editor for *Esquire* magazine. His work has appeared in numerous other publications, including the *New York Times* and *New York Magazine*. He is the author of *Just Folks: Visitin' with Carolina People; You Can't Live on Radishes; The World's Number One, Flat-Out, All-Time-Great Stock Car Racing Book; Where's Mark Twain When We Really Need Him?; From Whalebone to Hot House;* and *Bitter Blood*. He lives with his wife, Linda, on a farm near Asheboro, in Randolph County.